Southern Living

THE SOUTHERN

CAKE

BOOK

Southern Living

THE SOUTHERN CAKE BOOK

Oxmoor House

Welcome!

For a really special dessert, something that will delight your family and friends, look no further than a cake. Cakes are the frosted equivalent of happiness and cheer—the perfect celebration sweet. They offer a slice of bliss, and we Southerners know all about taking our time to enjoy the sweeter side of life, one bite at a time.

Nostalgic and old-fashioned yet wonderfully fresh, every layer cake, pound cake, cupcake, and more comes with the *Southern Living* stamp of approval. The confections found on these pages are bound to be the next beloved birthday cake, congratulatory torte, or weeknight indulgence that you'll want to share again and again. With easy-to-follow techniques, plus kitchen secrets and tips, any home baker can make a Southern cake worth bragging about!

From sun-ripened peaches to freshly gathered pecans, the delicious ingredients used in these recipes take the cakes to heavenly heights. Rich buttercreams, lofty meringues, and delicate glazes add flair. From crowd-pleasing flavors like red velvet and caramel to decidedly Southern favorites like ambrosia and Mississippi mud, there's a from-scratch sweet waiting to be discovered just a few pages away!

Allison E Cox

Editor

Contents

Bake with Love

Become a better baker with the help of these insider tips and techniques for foolproof cake baking.

■ **Carefully read through the entire recipe,** and prepare any special ingredients, such as chopped fruits and nuts, before mixing the batter.

■ **Measure accurately.** Be sure to use dry measuring cups for flour and sugar. Spoon flour into the cups, and lightly level with a knife. Extra sugar or leavening causes a cake to fall; extra flour makes it dry.

■ **Make sure to use the flour called for in the recipe,** because it affects both the flavor and texture. All-purpose flour is a blend of hard and soft wheat, used for most baking. Cake flour is milled from soft wheat and gives cakes a tender, fine crumb.

■ **When a recipe calls for softened butter, it's important that the butter is indeed soft** so it can cream in with the sugar or blend easily into the batter. Soften butter at room temperature for 30 minutes. Avoid softening the butter in the microwave, as it can melt quickly.

■ **Add eggs, one at a time, beating just until the yolk disappears.** Overbeating the eggs may cause the batter to overflow the sides of the pan when baked or create a fragile crust that crumbles and separates from the cake as it cools.

■ **Always add the dry ingredients alternately with the liquid,** beginning and ending with the dry ingredients, to prevent the batter from curdling. Mix just until blended after each addition. Overmixing the batter once the flour has been added creates a tough, rubbery cake.

■ **Grease cake pans with solid vegetable shortening,** such as Crisco, and always dust with flour—a slippery surface keeps the batter from rising to its full volume.

■ **Use an oven thermometer** to check your oven's temperature for accuracy. Many home ovens bake hotter or cooler than the temperatures to which they're set.

■ **Place the cake pan in the center of the oven, and keep the door closed** until the minimum baking time has elapsed. If the cake requires more baking, gently close the oven door as soon as possible after testing to prevent jarring and loss of heat—both can cause a cake to fall if it's not done.

SEPARATING EGGS

1. Crack egg. Gently transfer yolk back and forth between shell halves, allowing white to drip into bowl.

2. Gently place egg yolk in a second bowl.

3. Check egg white for traces of yolk; if clean, transfer white into a third bowl.

FOLDING

1. Place one-third of egg whites into batter.

2. Fold egg whites up and through center of batter.

3. Fold batter until there are no visible signs of egg whites.

CREAMING

1. For maximum volume, start with all ingredients at room temperature.

2. Beat softened butter and sugar for 5 to 7 minutes at medium speed with an electric mixer.

3. Mixture should be very light and fluffy.

BAKING AND LEVELING

1. Test for doneness by inserting a wooden pick into the center. It should come out clean, with no batter clinging to it.

2. Using a long serrated knife, cut off top in a sawing motion, keeping the knife parallel to the surface.

3. Discard cake top or save for another use.

Frost with Flair

Learn the tricks and secrets for turning a delectable cake into a showstopping masterpiece. Dollop, slather, and pipe your way to frosted perfection!

THE BASIC FROSTED CAKE

1. Stack up cake layers and frosting on a rotating pedestal. Place pieces of waxed paper or parchment under sides for easy cleanup.

2. Dollop frosting on top of cake, and smooth out a thin layer over sides and top.

3. Once cake is covered in a thin layer of frosting, refrigerate for 30 minutes so frosting sets and cake is stable.

4. Dollop more frosting onto cake, and smooth out over sides and top. Serve as is, or use as a canvas for a frosting flourish.

OUR FAVORITE DECORATING TIPS

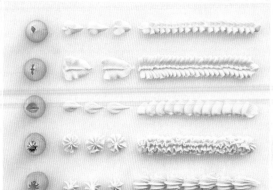

‹ *Leaf tip #352*

‹ *Leaf tip #70*

‹ *Petal tip #104*

‹ *Closed-Star tip #30*

‹ *Open-Star tip #20*

The Fanciest Frosting Flourishes

BASKETWEAVE

1. Using a basketweave tip, pipe a few vertical lines 1½ inches apart onto cake side.

2. Pipe horizontal bars over each vertical line, leaving ½-inch gaps in-between.

3. Repeat vertical lines and horizontal bars around cake sides.

CASCADING PETALS

1. Using a large round tip, pipe 5 large dots in a vertical row down side of cake.

2. With an offset spatula, spread dots outward to one side.

3. Repeat dots, spreading them in the same direction around cake sides.

RUFFLES

1. Using a large petal tip, pipe frosting back and forth into a column, starting from cake bottom and working upward.

2. Repeat column of ruffles.

3. Repeat effect around sides of cake.

ROSES

1. Using a large open-star tip, pipe frosting into a circle, creating a rose.

2. Repeat rose around sides of cake.

3. Repeat rose on top of cake.

Serve with Style

Even the humblest of cakes can be a party-worthy stunner when expertly showcased using these easy ideas.

1. In Full Bloom

Pick a few posies from the garden, and place around the base of a cake or on top. Be sure to use edible ones such as roses, tulips, lavender, violas, or geraniums.

2. Heirloom Finery

Pretty porcelain plates, silver dessert forks, and vintage cake servers make all the difference when doling out homemade slices. Borrow them from grandma or pick a few up at antiques stores or flea markets.

3. Put on a Pedestal

Any cake becomes instantly prettier on a pedestal or platter. Choose one with a ruffled edge in a fun hue, or of great height to make your cake oh-so-special.

4. Berry Beautiful

Surround your cake with nature's sweetest offering— fresh fruit! Whole fruit will last the longest, so choose those small in size like berries, kumquats, or cherries.

A BIT OF CAKE

Buttermilk-Glazed Mini Fig Cakes

MAKES: 20 MINI CAKES · HANDS-ON: 15 MIN. · TOTAL: 1 HOUR, 50 MIN.

Muffin pans make the perfect baking vessels for these little fig cakes. Gussy them up by spooning a dollop or piping a silver dollar of hard sauce on top and then garnish them with halved fresh figs, fresh herbs, or even pecan halves.

1. Preheat oven to 350°. Stir together flour and next 5 ingredients in a large bowl. Gradually add oil, beating at medium speed with an electric mixer until blended. Add eggs, 1 at a time, beating until blended. Add buttermilk and vanilla, beating until blended. Fold in preserves and pecans.

2. Spoon batter into 2 (12-cup) lightly greased (with cooking spray) muffin pans, filling 20 muffin cups about three-fourths full.

3. Bake at 350° for 15 to 18 minutes or until a wooden pick inserted in center comes out clean. Cool in pans on wire racks 10 minutes. Invert cakes onto wire racks. Cool completely (about 45 minutes).

4. Drizzle cakes with Buttermilk Glaze. Cool 10 minutes. Pipe Vanilla Hard Sauce onto warm cakes, and serve.

Buttermilk Glaze

Bring ½ cup sugar, ¼ cup buttermilk, 4 Tbsp. butter, 2 tsp. cornstarch, and ¼ tsp. baking soda to a boil in a small saucepan over medium heat, stirring often. Immediately remove mixture from heat, and cool 10 minutes. Stir in 1½ tsp. vanilla extract. Makes about ¾ cup.

Vanilla Hard Sauce

Split 1 vanilla bean lengthwise, and scrape seeds into a large bowl. Stir in 2 cups powdered sugar. Beat 1 cup softened butter into sugar mixture at medium speed with an electric mixer until blended. Makes about 1½ cups.

INGREDIENTS

2 cups all-purpose flour

1 cup sugar

1 tsp. baking soda

1 tsp. table salt

1 tsp. ground cinnamon

1 tsp. ground cloves

1 cup vegetable oil

3 large eggs

1 cup buttermilk

1 tsp. vanilla extract

1 cup fig preserves

½ cup chopped toasted pecans

Vegetable cooking spray

Buttermilk Glaze

Vanilla Hard Sauce

Garnishes: fresh rosemary sprigs, fresh fig halves

½ cup butter, softened

1 cup sugar

2 large eggs,
at room temperature

1¼ cups all-purpose flour

1 tsp. baking soda

1 tsp. vanilla extract

½ tsp. table salt

½ tsp. ground ginger

½ tsp. ground cinnamon

1 (15-oz.) can sweet potatoes,
drained and mashed

⅓ cup buttermilk

Vegetable cooking spray

½ cup chopped pecans, toasted

Caramel-Pecan Sauce

Vanilla ice cream (optional)

Heavy cream (optional)

Baby Sweet Potato Cakes
with Sticky Caramel-Pecan Sauce

MAKES: 12 MINI CAKES · **HANDS-ON:** 25 MIN. · **TOTAL:** 45 MIN.

1. Preheat oven to 350°. Beat butter and sugar at medium speed with an electric mixer until smooth. Add eggs, 1 at a time, beating until blended after each addition.

2. Combine flour and baking soda. Gradually add half of flour mixture to butter mixture, beating at low speed until blended, stopping to scrape down sides as needed. Add remaining half of flour mixture, and beat until blended. Add vanilla and next 5 ingredients, beating at medium speed until smooth. Spoon batter into a 12-cup lightly greased (with cooking spray) muffin pan, filling two-thirds full.

3. Bake at 350° for 15 minutes or until a wooden pick inserted in center comes out clean. Cool in pan on a wire rack 5 minutes. Remove warm cakes from pan, and sprinkle with toasted pecans. Top each cake with 2½ Tbsp. Caramel-Pecan Sauce. Serve with vanilla ice cream or ice-cold heavy cream, if desired.

Caramel-Pecan Sauce

Cook ½ cup butter and ¾ cup firmly packed light brown sugar in a medium nonstick skillet over medium heat 2 to 3 minutes or until butter melts and sugar dissolves. Whisk in 1 cup heavy cream and ½ tsp. coffee granules. Bring mixture to a light boil, stirring constantly. Turn off heat, and let stand on cooktop until slightly cool, stirring often. Makes about 2 cups.

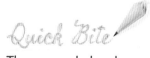

Quick Bite

These sweet little cakes can be turned into cupcakes with just a flip of the cake and a slather of frosting. We recommend Cream Cheese Frosting on page 43. Drizzle a little caramel sauce over the frosting.

Cherries Jubilee Cakes

MAKES: 10 CAKES · HANDS-ON: 45 MIN. · TOTAL: 2 HOURS

No one will ever guess that these elegant little cakes came from a box of white cake mix and a couple of cans of cherries.

1. Preheat oven to 350°. Drain cherries, reserving ¾ cup liquid from cans. Coarsely chop ½ cup cherries, and drain well, pressing between paper towels to squeeze out excess juice.

2. Prepare cake mix batter according to package directions; stir chopped cherries into batter. Lightly grease 2 (6-cup) jumbo muffin pans with cooking spray. Spoon batter into 10 muffin cups, filling two-thirds full.

3. Bake at 350° for 17 to 19 minutes or until a wooden pick inserted in center comes out clean. Cool in pans on wire racks 10 minutes; remove from pans to wire racks, and cool completely (about 45 minutes).

4. Meanwhile, bring remaining cherries, granulated sugar, and reserved cherry liquid to a boil in a saucepan over medium-high heat. Reduce heat to low, and simmer, stirring constantly, 1 minute. Stir together cornstarch and 2 Tbsp. water until combined. Quickly stir cornstarch mixture into cherry mixture, and cook, stirring often, 2 minutes or until mixture begins to thicken. Remove from heat, and cool 15 minutes.

5. Hollow out a 2½-inch hole from the top of each cake. Top each with about 2 Tbsp. cherry mixture.

6. Spoon whipped topping into a medium bowl. Stir in brandy, if desired, just before serving. Dollop mixture over cakes. Serve immediately, or chill 24 hours.

NOTE: *We tested with Oregon Fruit Products Pitted Red Tart Cherries in Water.*

Quick Bite

Just a couple of Tbsp. of cherry brandy can take store-bought whipped topping to new heights and make your guests wonder if it was made from scratch.

INGREDIENTS

2 (14.5-oz.) cans pitted tart cherries in water

1 (15.25-oz.) package white cake mix

Vegetable cooking spray

¾ cup granulated sugar

3 Tbsp. cornstarch

1 (12-oz.) container frozen whipped topping, thawed

2 Tbsp. clear cherry brandy (optional)

Garnishes: powdered sugar

INGREDIENTS

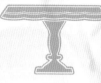

¾ cup golden raisins

⅓ cup dark rum

4 large eggs,
at room temperature

2 cups sugar

1 cup vegetable oil

2 tsp. vanilla extract

2 cups pureed roasted
sweet potatoes

3 cups all-purpose flour

1½ tsp. ground cinnamon

1 tsp. baking powder

1 tsp. baking soda

½ tsp. fine sea salt

½ tsp. ground nutmeg

¾ cup buttermilk

Vegetable cooking spray

Rum Glaze

½ cup finely chopped
toasted pecans

Rum-Glazed Sweet Potato Cakes

MAKES: 36 MINI CAKES · HANDS-ON: 40 MIN. · TOTAL: 1 HOUR, 15 MIN.

This mini Bundt cake recipe features pureed sweet potatoes, raisins, rum, and toasted pecans, along with cinnamon and nutmeg, and is a perfect pick-up treat for a holiday dessert party.

1. Preheat oven to 350°. Stir together first 2 ingredients. Let stand 30 minutes.

2. Meanwhile, beat eggs and sugar at high speed with an electric mixer 2 to 4 minutes or until thick and pale. Add oil and vanilla, beating at low speed just until blended. Add sweet potato puree, beating just until blended and stopping to scrape down sides as needed.

3. Sift together flour and next 5 ingredients; add to egg mixture alternately with buttermilk, beginning and ending with flour mixture. Beat at low speed just until blended after each addition. Drain raisins, reserving rum. Fold raisins into batter. Spoon batter into 3 (12-cavity) lightly greased (with cooking spray) mini fluted tube pans (¼-cup capacity), filling each three-fourths full.

4. Bake at 350° for 14 to 16 minutes or until a wooden pick inserted in center comes out clean. Cool in pans on lightly greased wire racks 5 minutes. Remove from pans to wire racks.

5. Pierce tops of cakes multiple times using a wooden pick. Dip top halves of cakes in Rum Glaze, and hold 1 to 2 seconds (to allow syrup to soak into cakes). Place, glazed sides up, on lightly greased racks. Sprinkle each cake with pecans.

Rum Glaze

Bring ½ cup brown sugar, ¼ cup butter, and 3 Tbsp. whipping cream to a boil in a heavy saucepan over medium-high heat. Boil, stirring constantly, 3 minutes or until mixture begins to thicken to a syrup-like consistency. Remove from heat; stir in reserved rum from cake recipe (about ¼ cup).

NOTE: *To puree roasted sweet potatoes, peel potatoes as soon as they are slightly cooled. Press pulp through a wire-mesh strainer with the back of a spoon. You'll need to roast about 1½ lb. potatoes for 2 cups puree.*

Praline Mini Cakes

MAKES: 12 MINI CAKES • HANDS-ON: 20 MIN. • TOTAL: 1 HOUR, 40 MIN.

1. Preheat oven to 350°. Generously grease 2 (6-cup) mini fluted tube pans with shortening (do not use cooking spray); lightly flour.

2. Beat cake mix and next 3 ingredients together at low speed with an electric mixer 30 seconds. Increase speed to medium, and beat 2 minutes, stopping to scrape down sides as needed. Fold in pecans and ½ cup toffee bits. Divide batter evenly among prepared cake pans.

3. Bake at 350° for 18 to 23 minutes or until a wooden pick inserted in center comes out clean. Cool in pans on wire racks 10 minutes; remove from pans to wire racks, and cool completely (about 45 minutes).

4. Drizzle about 1 Tbsp. Brown Sugar Icing over each cake. Store loosely covered at room temperature.

Brown Sugar Icing

Melt ¼ cup butter in a 1-qt. saucepan over medium-high heat. Stir in ½ cup brown sugar, 2 Tbsp. corn syrup, and 2 Tbsp. milk. Heat to rolling boil over medium-high heat, stirring frequently; remove from heat. Immediately beat in 1 cup powdered sugar and 1 tsp. vanilla extract with whisk until smooth.

Technique Tip

When making the Brown Sugar Icing, make sure to remove pan from heat just as soon as it comes to a boil. Remember to keep stirring the mixture while cooking to prevent the sugar from burning.

INGREDIENTS

Shortening

Flour

1 (15.25-oz.) package yellow cake mix

1 cup water

½ cup vegetable oil

3 large eggs

½ cup chopped pecans

½ cup toffee bits

Brown Sugar Icing

Garnish: ¼ cup toffee bits

INGREDIENTS

Shortening

Unsweetened cocoa

2¼ cups all-purpose flour

1 tsp. baking soda

½ tsp. table salt

½ cup boiling water

½ cup unsweetened Dutch
process baking cocoa

1 (8-oz.) container sour cream

2 cups sugar

1 cup butter, softened

1 tsp. vanilla extract

1 tsp. almond extract

3 large eggs

1 cup miniature semisweet
chocolate morsels

Almond Glaze

½ cup milk chocolate morsels

Garnishes: toasted flaked
coconut, coarsely chopped
unblanched whole almonds,
miniature semisweet
chocolate morsels

Almond-Coconut Mini Cakes

MAKES: 12 MINI CAKES · **HANDS-ON:** 30 MIN. · **TOTAL:** 1 HOUR, 50 MIN.

1. Preheat oven to 350°. Grease 2 (6-cup) mini fluted tube pans with shortening; lightly sprinkle with cocoa. Mix flour, baking soda, and salt in a medium-size bowl; set aside. Mix boiling water and ½ cup cocoa in a separate medium-size bowl; stir in sour cream until well blended. Set aside.

2. Beat sugar and butter at medium speed with an electric mixer until light and fluffy. Beat in vanilla and 1 tsp. almond extract. Beat in eggs, 1 at a time, until blended. Alternately add flour mixture and cocoa mixture at low speed, beating just until blended after each addition. Stir in miniature chocolate morsels. Divide batter evenly among prepared pans, filling each two-thirds full.

3. Bake at 350° for 20 to 25 minutes or until a wooden pick inserted in center comes out clean. Run knife around edges. Cool in pans on wire racks 10 minutes; remove from pans to wire racks, and cool completely (about 45 minutes).

4. Drizzle glaze over cakes. Place milk chocolate morsels in a zip-top plastic freezer bag; seal bag. Microwave on HIGH about 1 minute or until softened. Gently squeeze bag until chocolate is smooth; cut off tiny corner of bag. Squeeze bag to drizzle chocolate over cakes.

Almond Glaze

Mix 2 cups powdered sugar, 6 Tbsp. whipping cream, and ¼ tsp. almond extract in a small bowl until smooth.

Baby Pound Cakes

MAKES: 30 BABY POUND CAKES · HANDS-ON: 28 MIN. · TOTAL: 1 HOUR, 40 MIN.

Enjoy these pound cake bites for breakfast or as a late-night snack by the fire. Or split them and toast them with butter. Vanilla bean paste gives these cakes a sublime goodness. And just as with classic pound cake, we loved the crusty top edges on these, too.

1. Preheat oven to 350°. Beat butter and cream cheese at medium speed with an electric mixer about 2 minutes or until creamy. Gradually add granulated sugar, beating well, 5 to 7 minutes. Add eggs, 1 at a time, beating just until yellow disappears.

2. Combine flour and salt. Gradually add to butter mixture, beating at low speed just until blended; stir in vanilla and almond flavorings.

3. Spoon batter into 3 (12-cavity) lightly greased (with cooking spray) mini fluted tube pans (¼-cup capacity), filling each three-fourths full.

4. Bake at 350° for 20 minutes or until a wooden pick inserted in center comes out clean. Cool in pans on wire racks 10 minutes; remove from pans to wire racks, and cool completely (about 45 minutes).

Pound Cake Minis: Preheat oven to 350°. Make batter as described above. Place baking cups in 5 (24-cup) miniature muffin pans, skipping every other muffin cup in fifth pan. Coat cups with cooking spray. Spoon batter into cups, filling three-fourths full. Bake 16 to 18 minutes or until a wooden pick inserted in center comes out clean. Cool in pans on wire racks 10 minutes; remove from pans to wire racks, and cool completely. Makes about 9 dozen mini cakes.

NOTE: *The vanilla bean paste really does add a more distinct vanilla flavor to these cakes. You can find it at specialty food stores or order it online.*

INGREDIENTS

1½ cups butter, softened

1 (8-oz.) package cream cheese, softened

3 cups granulated sugar

6 large eggs

3 cups all-purpose flour

¼ tsp. table salt

1 Tbsp. vanilla bean paste or vanilla extract

½ tsp. almond extract

Paper baking cups (for minis)

Vegetable cooking spray

Garnish: powdered sugar or Powdered Sugar Glaze (page 182)

INGREDIENTS

6 (5- x 3-inch) disposable aluminum foil loaf pans

Vegetable cooking spray

2 cups sugar

½ cup butter, softened

½ cup canola oil

3 large eggs

2⅓ cups all-purpose flour

⅔ cup unsweetened cocoa

1 tsp. baking soda

1 tsp. table salt

½ tsp. ground cinnamon

⅔ cup whole buttermilk

2 cups grated unpeeled zucchini (about 2 medium)

1 (4-oz.) semisweet chocolate baking bar, finely chopped

2 tsp. vanilla extract

Chocolate Fudge Frosting

Garnishes: edible flowers, fresh zucchini strips

Chocolate Zucchini Cakes

MAKES: 6 (5- X 3-INCH) CAKES · HANDS-ON: 30 MIN. · TOTAL: 2 HOURS, 55 MIN.

Adding freshly grated zucchini to the batter yields luxuriously dense, moist results. The frosting sets up quickly, so prepare it after cooling the cakes.

1. Preheat oven to 350°. Lightly grease loaf pans with cooking spray.

2. Beat sugar, butter, and oil at medium speed with a heavy-duty electric stand mixer until light and fluffy. Add eggs, 1 at a time, beating just until blended after each addition. Sift together flour and next 4 ingredients; add to butter mixture alternately with buttermilk, beginning and ending with flour mixture. Beat at low speed just until blended after each addition. Stir zucchini and next 2 ingredients into batter until blended. Spoon batter into pans, filling two-thirds full.

3. Bake at 350° for 30 to 35 minutes or until a wooden pick inserted in center comes out clean. Cool in pans on wire racks 10 minutes; remove from pans to wire racks, and cool completely (about 1 hour).

4. Spoon hot Chocolate Fudge Frosting over cooled cakes (about ¼ cup each); cool completely (about 30 minutes).

Chocolate Fudge Frosting

Cook ⅓ cup butter, ⅓ cup unsweetened cocoa, and ⅓ cup milk in a large saucepan over medium heat, stirring constantly, 3 to 4 minutes or until butter melts. Remove from heat; whisk in ¼ cup sour cream and 2 tsp. vanilla until blended. Gradually add 3 cups powdered sugar, beating at medium speed with an electric mixer until smooth. Use immediately. Makes about 2 cups.

Quick Bite

For the pretty brown paper loaf pans pictured, look for mini paper loaf pans (4- x 2-inch) online or in baking stores. They are a little smaller than the foil pans, so you will get 7 to 8 cakes.

White Coconut Cupcakes

MAKES: 24 CUPCAKES • HANDS-ON: 15 MIN. • TOTAL: 1 HOUR, 35 MIN.

These simple cupcakes use a white cake mix enhanced with buttermilk, butter, and flavoring extracts. A topping of Coconut Buttercream and flaked coconut turns them into a snowy dream.

1. Preheat oven to 350°. Beat first 6 ingredients at low speed with an electric mixer just until dry ingredients are moistened. Increase speed to medium, and beat 2 minutes or until batter is smooth, stopping to scrape down sides as needed.

2. Place paper baking cups in 2 (12-cup) muffin pans, and coat with cooking spray; spoon batter evenly into cups, filling each two-thirds full.

3. Bake at 350° for 25 minutes or until a wooden pick inserted in center comes out clean. Cool in pans on wire racks 10 minutes; remove from pans to wire racks, and cool completely (about 45 minutes).

4. Spread evenly with Coconut Buttercream, and sprinkle with sweetened flaked coconut.

Coconut Buttercream

Beat ½ cup softened butter and 1 (3-oz.) package cream cheese at medium speed with an electric mixer until creamy. Gradually add 1 (16-oz.) package powdered sugar, beating at low speed until blended. Increase speed to medium, and slowly add ¼ cup cream of coconut and 1 tsp. vanilla extract, beating until smooth. Makes 3 cups.

Technique Tip

We call for using a mixer, but you can stir these together by hand with great results. Because the mixer adds more air to the batter, you'll end up with 17 cakes rather than 24 when you stir them by hand. For testing purposes only, we used Pillsbury Moist Supreme Classic White Cake Mix.

INGREDIENTS

1 (18.25-oz.) package white cake mix with pudding

1¼ cups buttermilk

¼ cup butter, melted

2 large eggs

2 tsp. vanilla extract

½ tsp. almond extract

Paper baking cups

Vegetable cooking spray

Coconut Buttercream

1 cup sweetened flaked coconut

INGREDIENTS

1¾ cups plus 2 Tbsp. sugar

1⅓ cups all-purpose flour

¼ tsp. table salt

2 tsp. lemon juice

½ tsp. vanilla extract

½ tsp. light rum

¼ tsp. orange extract

1¾ cups egg whites
(about 13 to 15 large eggs)

¾ tsp. cream of tartar

12 (2½- x 2-inch) muffin-size
paper baking molds

Lemon Curd Filling

Cream Cheese Frosting
(page 43)

Garnish: lemon zest

Lemon Curd-Filled Angel Food Cupcakes

MAKES: 12 CUPCAKES · **HANDS-ON:** 30 MIN. · **TOTAL:** 1 HOUR, 32 MIN.

1. Preheat oven to 375°. Sift together sugar, flour, and salt in a bowl. Combine lemon juice, vanilla extract, rum, and orange extract.

2. Beat egg whites and cream of tartar at high speed with a heavy-duty electric stand mixer until stiff peaks form; gently transfer egg white mixture to a large bowl. Gradually fold in sugar mixture with a large spatula, ⅓ cup at a time, folding just until blended after each addition. Fold in lemon juice mixture.

3. Arrange 12 (2½- x 2-inch) muffin-size paper baking molds on an aluminum foil-lined baking sheet; spoon batter into baking molds, filling almost completely full.

4. Bake at 375° for 17 to 19 minutes or until a wooden pick inserted in centers comes out clean. Transfer to a wire rack, and cool completely (about 45 minutes)

5. Make a small hole in top of each cupcake using the handle of a wooden spoon. Spoon Lemon Curd Filling into a zip-top plastic freezer bag. Snip 1 corner of bag to make a tiny hole. Pipe a generous amount of filling into each cupcake. Spread Cream Cheese Frosting on tops of cupcakes.

Lemon Curd Filling

Stir together 1 (10-oz.) jar lemon curd and ⅓ cup sour cream until blended. Cover and chill until ready to use. Makes 1¼ cups.

Chocolate Extreme Cupcakes

MAKES: 12 CUPCAKES · HANDS-ON: 25 MIN. · TOTAL: 1 HOUR, 50 MIN.

What makes these cupcakes extreme? They're huge! Plus, they're loaded with two types of chocolate and they're topped with Whipped Chocolate Frosting for an irresistible and indulgent treat.

1. Preheat oven to 350°. Place jumbo baking cups in 2 (6-cup) jumbo muffin pans. Coat cups with cooking spray.

2. Mix flour, baking soda, and ½ tsp. salt in a small bowl; set aside. Microwave baking chocolates in a small microwave-safe bowl at HIGH 1 to 2 minutes, stirring once, until softened and chocolate can be stirred smooth.

3. Beat 1 cup butter at medium speed with an electric mixer until creamy. Gradually add brown sugar and granulated sugar, beating well. Add eggs, 1 at a time, beating until blended after each addition. Add melted chocolate and 1 tsp. vanilla, beating well. Add flour mixture alternately with butter-milk, beating at low speed after each addition until blended. Spoon into cups, filling three-fourths full.

4. Bake at 350° for 30 minutes or until a wooden pick inserted in center comes out clean. Cool in pans on wire racks 10 minutes; remove from pans to wire racks, and cool completely (about 45 minutes). Spread Whipped Chocolate Frosting evenly over cupcakes.

Whipped Chocolate Frosting

Microwave 1 cup semisweet chocolate morsels in a small microwave-safe bowl at HIGH 1 to 2 minutes, stirring once, until softened and chocolate can be stirred smooth. Beat ½ cup softened butter at medium speed with an electric mixer until creamy. Add 1 (16-oz.) package powdered sugar alternately with melted chocolate and ½ cup whipping cream, beating at low speed after each addition until blended. Stir in 2 tsp. vanilla extract and dash of table salt.

INGREDIENTS

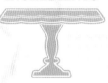

12 jumbo paper baking cups

Vegetable cooking spray

2 cups all-purpose flour

1 tsp. baking soda

½ tsp. table salt

3 oz. unsweetened baking chocolate

3 oz. semisweet baking chocolate

1 cup butter, softened

1 cup packed brown sugar

½ cup granulated sugar

4 large eggs

1 tsp. vanilla extract

1 cup buttermilk

Whipped Chocolate Frosting

INGREDIENTS

⅓ cup butter, softened

⅔ cup sugar

2 large eggs

1 cup all-purpose flour

⅓ cup unsweetened cocoa

¼ tsp. table salt

½ cup sour cream

¾ tsp. baking soda

1 (4-oz.) semisweet
chocolate baking bar,
chopped and divided

12 paper baking cups

Vegetable cooking spray

Marshmallow Frosting

⅓ cup roasted glazed
pecan pieces

Mississippi Mud Cupcakes

MAKES: 12 CUPCAKES · **HANDS-ON:** 20 MIN. · **TOTAL:** 1 HOUR, 55 MIN.

1. Preheat oven to 350°. Beat butter at medium speed with an electric mixer until fluffy; gradually add sugar, beating well. Add eggs, 1 at a time, beating just until blended.

2. Combine flour, cocoa, and salt. Stir together sour cream and baking soda. Add flour mixture to butter mixture alternately with sour cream mixture, beginning and ending with flour mixture. Beat at low speed just until blended after each addition. Stir in half of chopped chocolate.

3. Place paper baking cups in a 12-cup muffin pan, and coat with cooking spray; spoon batter into cups, filling two-thirds full.

4. Bake at 350° for 18 to 20 minutes or until a wooden pick inserted in center comes out clean. Cool in pan on wire rack 10 minutes; remove from pan to wire rack, and cool completely (about 45 minutes). Pipe or frost Marshmallow Frosting onto cupcakes; sprinkle with pecans and remaining chopped chocolate.

Marshmallow Frosting

Beat together ½ (8-oz.) package softened cream cheese, ¼ cup softened butter, 1 (7-oz.) jar marshmallow crème, and 2 tsp. vanilla extract at medium speed with an electric mixer until creamy. Gradually add 2½ cups powdered sugar, beating at low speed until blended and smooth.

Technique Tip

This frosting is so soft and cloud-like, you can dollop a spoonful onto each cupcake instead of piping.

Lane Cupcakes

MAKES: 24 CUPCAKES • HANDS-ON: 20 MIN. • TOTAL: 1 HOUR, 45 MIN.

These handheld treats are inspired by the iconic Southern layer cake that bears the same name. The Lane Cake has been around for more than 100 years. These cupcakes boast a white frosting and a dollop of filling, while the more traditional layer cake (page 76) is sandwiched with filling that dribbles down the sides.

1. Preheat oven to 350°. Place paper baking cups in 2 (12-cup) muffin pans, and coat with cooking spray.

2. Mix flour, baking powder, and salt in a medium bowl. Mix milk, vanilla, almond extract, and egg whites in a small bowl. Beat sugar and butter at medium speed with an electric mixer until light and fluffy. Add flour mixture alternately with milk mixture, beginning and ending with flour mixture. Beat at low speed just until blended after each addition. Beat at low speed 1 minute. Spoon batter into cups, filling two-thirds full.

3. Bake at 350° for 25 to 28 minutes or until a wooden pick inserted in center comes out clean. Cool in pans on wire racks 10 minutes; remove from pans to wire racks. Brush bourbon over cupcakes. Cool completely (about 45 minutes).

4. Mix coconut-pecan frosting and raisins in a medium bowl. Spread white frosting evenly over cupcakes. Make slight indentation in frosting in center of each cupcake; spoon about 1 tsp. coconut-pecan frosting mixture in each indentation. Top each with a cherry.

INGREDIENTS

Paper baking cups

Vegetable cooking spray

3 cups all-purpose flour

2 tsp. baking powder

1/2 tsp. table salt

1 cup milk

1 tsp. vanilla extract

1 tsp. almond extract

5 large egg whites

1 3/4 cups sugar

1 cup butter, softened

2 Tbsp. bourbon

2/3 cup ready-to-spread coconut-pecan frosting (from 16-oz. container)

3/4 cup mixed jumbo raisins

1 (12-oz.) container fluffy white frosting

24 maraschino cherries with stems

INGREDIENTS

1½ cups semisweet chocolate morsels

½ cup butter, softened

1 (16-oz.) package light brown sugar

3 large eggs

2 cups all-purpose flour

1 tsp. baking soda

½ tsp. table salt

1 (8-oz.) container sour cream

1 cup hot water

2 tsp. vanilla extract

Paper baking cups

Browned Butter-Cinnamon-Cream Cheese Frosting

Garnish: chocolate curls

Chocolate Velvet Cupcakes

MAKES: 36 CUPCAKES · HANDS-ON: 15 MIN. · TOTAL: 1 HOUR, 25 MIN.

Chocolate Velvet Cupcakes are topped with a to-die-for Browned Butter-Cinnamon-Cream Cheese Frosting for an irresistible bite-size dessert.

1. Preheat oven to 350°. Microwave morsels in a microwave-safe bowl at HIGH 1 to 1½ minutes or until melted and smooth, stirring at 30-second intervals.

2. Beat butter and sugar at medium speed with an electric mixer until well blended (about 5 minutes). Add eggs, 1 at a time, beating just until blended after each addition. Add melted chocolate; beat until blended.

3. Sift together flour, baking soda, and salt. Gradually add to chocolate mixture alternately with sour cream, beginning and ending with flour mixture. Beat at low speed just until blended after each addition. Gradually add hot water in a slow, steady stream, beating at low speed just until blended. Stir in vanilla.

4. Place 36 paper baking cups in 3 (12-cup) muffin pans; spoon batter into cups, filling three-fourths full.

5. Bake at 350° for 18 to 20 minutes or until a wooden pick inserted in centers comes out clean. Cool in pans on wire racks 10 minutes; remove from pans to wire racks, and cool completely (about 45 minutes).

6. Pipe frosting onto cupcakes.

Browned Butter-Cinnamon-Cream Cheese Frosting

Cook ½ cup butter in a small heavy saucepan over medium heat, stirring constantly, 6 to 8 minutes or until butter begins to turn golden brown. Immediately remove from heat. Pour butter into a bowl. Cover and chill 1 hour or until butter is cool and begins to solidify. Beat butter and 2 (8-oz.) packages softened cream cheese at medium speed with an electric mixer until creamy; gradually add 2 (16-oz.) packages powdered sugar, beating until light and fluffy. Stir in 1 tsp. ground cinnamon and 2 tsp. vanilla extract. Makes 5 cups.

Sweet Potato-
Pecan Cupcakes
with Cream Cheese Frosting

MAKES: 24 CUPCAKES • HANDS-ON: 15 MIN. • TOTAL: 1 HOUR, 55 MIN.

Mashed sweet potatoes give the cupcakes extra moistness, while cinnamon and nutmeg spice up this traditionally sweet dessert. A simple cream cheese frosting and a sprinkle of chopped pecans are all that's needed on top.

1. Preheat oven to 350°. Place aluminum foil baking cups in 2 (12-cup) muffin pans, and coat with cooking spray.

2. Beat sugar and butter at medium speed with an electric mixer until blended. Add eggs, 1 at a time, beating until blended after each addition.

3. Whisk together mashed sweet potatoes, orange juice, and vanilla extract. Combine flour and next 5 ingredients. Add flour mixture to sugar mixture alternately with sweet potato mixture, beginning and ending with flour mixture. Beat at low speed just until blended after each addition. Fold in toasted pecans. Spoon batter into cups, filling two-thirds full.

4. Bake at 350° for 28 to 30 minutes or until a wooden pick inserted in center comes out clean. Cool in pans on wire racks 10 minutes; remove from pans to wire racks, and cool completely (about 45 minutes). Spread cupcakes evenly with Cream Cheese Frosting.

Cream Cheese Frosting

Beat 1 (8-oz.) package softened cream cheese and ½ cup softened butter at medium speed with an electric mixer until fluffy. Gradually add 1 (16-oz.) package powdered sugar, beating at low speed until blended; add 1 tsp. vanilla extract, beating until blended. Makes 3½ cups.

INGREDIENTS

Aluminum foil baking cups

Vegetable cooking spray

2 cups sugar

1 cup butter, softened

4 large eggs

1 (16-oz.) can mashed sweet potatoes

⅔ cup orange juice

1 tsp. vanilla extract

3 cups all-purpose flour

1 tsp. baking powder

1 tsp. ground cinnamon

½ tsp. baking soda

½ tsp. ground nutmeg

¼ tsp. table salt

1 cup coarsely chopped toasted pecans

Cream Cheese Frosting

Garnish: coarsely chopped pecans

Paper baking cups

Vegetable cooking spray

1 (18.25-oz.) package
white cake mix

1¼ cups Belgian-style
wheat ale beer

⅓ cup vegetable oil

2 large egg whites

1 large whole egg

¼ tsp. ground coriander

¼ tsp. ground ginger

1 tsp. grated orange zest

Orange-Ale Frosting

Garnish: 24 small
orange wedges

Over-the-Moon White Ale Cupcakes

MAKES: 24 CUPCAKES · **HANDS-ON:** 30 MIN. · **TOTAL:** 1 HOUR, 50 MIN.

A fun take on a Belgian white ale topped with the popular orange-slice garnish, these cupcakes start with cake mix and amp up the flavor with beer, orange, and ginger.

1. Preheat oven to 350°. Place paper baking cups in 2 (12-cup) muffin pans, and coat with cooking spray.

2. Beat cake mix, 1¼ cups beer, oil, egg whites, egg, coriander, and ginger at low speed with an electric mixer 30 seconds. Increase speed to medium, and beat 2 minutes, stopping to scrape down sides as needed. Stir in 1 tsp. orange zest. Spoon batter into cups, filling two-thirds full.

3. Bake at 350° for 18 to 23 minutes or until a wooden pick inserted in center comes out clean. Cool in pans on wire racks 10 minutes; remove from pans to wire racks, and cool completely (about 45 minutes).

4. Spread frosting evenly over cupcakes. Just before serving, garnish each with an orange wedge. Store loosely covered in refrigerator.

Orange-Ale Frosting

Beat 6 cups powdered sugar, ½ cup softened butter, 1 tsp. grated orange zest, ¼ cup Belgian-style wheat ale beer, and 1 Tbsp. orange juice at medium speed with an electric mixer until smooth and creamy.

Quick Bite

With its mild flavor, white ale is the perfect beer for baking. Feel free to try lemon zest in place of the orange for both the cake and frosting, if desired.

Lemon-Rosemary Cornmeal Madeleines

MAKES: 4 DOZEN · HANDS-ON: 14 MIN. · TOTAL: 1 HOUR, 44 MIN.

A simple lemon glaze saturates these light sponge cakes and makes them memorable.

1. Whisk together cornmeal mix, flour, and granulated sugar in a large bowl. Add buttermilk, melted butter, eggs, lemon zest, and rosemary. Whisk together just until blended. Cover; refrigerate batter 30 minutes.

2. Preheat oven to 400°. Spoon batter into lightly greased (with shortening) and floured shiny madeleine pans, filling three-fourths full.

3. Bake at 400°, in batches, 15 to 17 minutes or until golden brown. Remove from pans immediately; let cool slightly. Dip both sides of each madeleine in Lemon Glaze; cool on wire rack, scalloped side up. Let stand until glaze sets.

Lemon Glaze

Whisk together 2⅔ cups powdered sugar, ¼ cup fresh lemon juice, and ⅓ cup milk in a medium bowl; set aside.

Serving Secret

Madeleines are sweet one by one, but they are quite the showstopper when served en masse. Arrange them in a circular pattern on a platter or pedestal with ruffled edges pointing outward. Pile them up as you circle around so they look like a wreath.

INGREDIENTS

2 cups self-rising white cornmeal mix

½ cup all-purpose flour

⅓ cup granulated sugar

1½ cups buttermilk

½ cup butter, melted

2 large eggs, lightly beaten

1 Tbsp. lemon zest

1 Tbsp. finely chopped fresh rosemary

Shortening

Lemon Glaze

INGREDIENTS

1 cup all-purpose flour

½ tsp. baking powder

½ tsp. baking soda

½ tsp. table salt

1 cup graham cracker crumbs

½ cup butter, softened

½ cup granulated sugar

½ cup firmly packed
light brown sugar

1 large egg

1 tsp. vanilla extract

1 (8-oz.) container
sour cream

Parchment paper

Marshmallow Filling

1 (12-oz.) package semisweet
chocolate morsels

2 tsp. shortening

Toppings: chopped roasted
salted pecans, chopped
crystallized ginger, sea salt

Swoon Pies

MAKES: 12 SWOON PIES · HANDS-ON: 45 MIN. · TOTAL: 2 HOURS, 40 MIN.

Swoon Pies are our take on the iconic marshmallow-filled pastry. This one has tender graham cookies dipped in chocolate and a few special toppings.

1. Preheat oven to 350°. Sift together flour and next 3 ingredients in a medium bowl; stir in graham cracker crumbs.

2. Beat butter and next 2 ingredients at medium speed with a heavy-duty electric stand mixer until fluffy. Add egg and vanilla, beating until blended. Add flour mixture to butter mixture alternately with sour cream, beginning and ending with flour mixture. Beat at low speed until blended after each addition, stopping to scrape down sides as needed.

3. Drop batter by rounded tablespoonfuls 2 inches apart onto 2 parchment paper-lined baking sheets. Bake, in batches, at 350° for 13 to 15 minutes or until set and bottoms are golden brown. Remove cookies (on parchment paper) to wire racks, and cool completely (about 30 minutes).

4. Turn 12 cookies over, bottom sides up. Spread each with 1 heaping tablespoonful Marshmallow Filling. Top with remaining 12 cookies, bottom sides down, and press gently to spread filling to edges. Freeze on a parchment paper-lined baking sheet 30 minutes or until filling is set.

5. Place chocolate and shortening in a 2-cup glass measuring cup. Microwave at HIGH for 1 to 2 minutes, stirring every 30 seconds until melted and smooth. Meanwhile, remove cookies from freezer, and let stand 10 minutes. Dip half of each cookie sandwich into melted chocolate mixture. Place on parchment paper-lined baking sheet. Sprinkle with desired toppings, and freeze 10 minutes or until chocolate is set.

Marshmallow Filling

Beat ½ cup softened butter at medium speed with an electric mixer until creamy; gradually add 1 cup powdered sugar, beating well. Add 1 cup marshmallow crème and ½ tsp. vanilla extract, beating until well blended Makes about 1½ cups.

Full Swoon Pies: Increase semisweet chocolate morsels to 1 (16-oz.) package and shortening to 3 tsp. Prepare recipe as directed, dipping cookie sandwiches completely in chocolate mixture. (Use a fork to easily remove sandwiches from chocolate.)

Petits Fours Presents

MAKES: 40 SERVINGS · **HANDS-ON:** 1 HOUR, 15 MIN. · **TOTAL:** 5 HOURS, 30 MIN.

1. Preheat oven to 325°. Beat butter at medium speed with an electric mixer until creamy. Gradually add sugar and marzipan; beat 5 minutes or until light and fluffy. Add eggs, 1 at a time, beating until blended after each addition.

2. Combine flour, baking powder, and salt; gradually add to butter mixture alternately with sour cream, beginning and ending with flour mixture. Beat at low speed just until blended after each addition, stopping to scrape down sides as needed. Stir in vanilla. Pour batter into a greased (with shortening) and floured 13- x 9-inch pan.

3. Bake at 325° for 55 minutes or until a wooden pick inserted in center comes out clean. Cool in pan on a wire rack 20 minutes; remove from pan to wire rack, and cool completely (about 1 hour).

4. Trim crusts from all surfaces, making sure top of cake is flat. Slice cake in half horizontally. Spread cut side of bottom half with strawberry jam; replace top half. Cover; freeze 1 hour or until firm.

5. Cut cake into 40 (1½-inch) squares; brush away loose crumbs. Place squares 2 inches apart on wire racks in jelly-roll pans. Pour Petits Fours Glaze over cake squares, completely covering top and sides. Spoon up all excess glaze; continue pouring glaze until all cakes have been covered. Let stand 1 hour or until glaze dries completely.

6. Trim any excess glaze from bottom of each cake square. Spoon Quick Almond Buttercream into a piping bag fitted with a small round tip, and decorate as desired.

Petits Fours Glaze

Beat 10 cups powdered sugar, ¼ cup meringue powder, 1 cup plus 2 Tbsp. half-and-half, and 2 tsp. almond extract at medium speed with an electric mixer until smooth.

NOTE: *We tested with Wilton Meringue Powder, which can be found at craft and cake-decorating stores.*

Quick Almond Buttercream

Beat ½ cup softened butter at medium speed with an electric mixer until creamy; gradually add 2 cups powdered sugar, beating until light and fluffy. Add 2 Tbsp. half-and-half and ½ tsp. almond extract; beat 1 minute. Stir in food coloring paste, if desired.

INGREDIENTS

1¼ cups butter, softened

2 cups sugar

1 (7-oz.) package marzipan (almond paste)

6 large eggs

3 cups all-purpose flour

½ tsp. baking powder

½ tsp. table salt

½ cup sour cream

1 tsp. vanilla extract

Shortening

1 cup strawberry jam

Petits Fours Glaze

Quick Almond Buttercream

INGREDIENTS

Shortening

Wax paper

¾ cup butter, softened

2 (8-oz.) cans almond paste

1½ cups sugar

8 large eggs

1½ cups all-purpose flour

1 (12-oz.) can apricot filling*

Chocolate Ganache

Garnishes: almond slices, dried apricots

Chocolate-Almond Petits Fours

MAKES: 36 PETIT FOURS • **HANDS-ON:** 20 MIN. • **TOTAL:** 1 HOUR, 55 MIN.

Perfect for birthdays and showers, these miniature cakes are simple and elegant. Plus, you can make and freeze them ahead for easy entertaining.

1. Preheat oven to 400°. Grease (with shortening) bottom and sides of 2 (15- x 10-inch) jelly-roll pans, and line with wax paper; grease (with shortening) and flour wax paper. Set aside.

2. Beat butter and almond paste at medium speed with an electric mixer until creamy. Gradually add sugar, beating well. Add eggs, 1 at a time, beating after each addition. Stir in flour, and spread batter into prepared pans.

3. Bake at 400° for 8 to 10 minutes. Cool in pans on wire racks 10 minutes; remove from pans to wire racks, and cool completely (about 1 hour).

4. Turn 1 cake out onto a flat surface; remove and discard wax paper, and spread with apricot filling. Top with remaining cake, and cut with a 1½-inch round cutter.

5. Place cakes on a wire rack in a large shallow pan. Using a squeeze bottle, coat top and sides with warm Chocolate Ganache. (Spoon up excess frosting that drips through rack; reheat and refill bottle, and use to continue frosting cakes.) Chill cakes at least 30 minutes. Freeze up to 3 months.

*1 (10-oz.) jar apricot spreadable fruit may be substituted for canned apricot filling.

Chocolate Ganache

Microwave 1 cup whipping cream in a 2-cup glass measuring cup at HIGH 2 minutes. Add 2 cups semisweet chocolate morsels, stirring until melted. Makes 2 cups.

Heavenly Angel Food Cake

MAKES: 15 SERVINGS · HANDS-ON: 15 MIN. · TOTAL: 1 HOUR, 50 MIN.

This classic angel food cake is the perfect dessert base for your next party. Cut the finished cake into single-serve portions for petits fours, or frost the whole cake to make a sheet cake.

1. Preheat oven to 375°. Line bottom and sides of a 13- x 9-inch pan with aluminum foil, allowing 2 to 3 inches to extend over sides of pan. (Do not grease pan or foil.) Sift together first 3 ingredients.

2. Beat egg whites and cream of tartar at high speed with a heavy-duty electric stand mixer until stiff peaks form. Gradually fold in sugar mixture, ⅓ cup at a time, folding just until blended after each addition. Fold in vanilla and lemon juice. Spoon batter into prepared pan. (Pan will be very full. The batter will reach almost to the top of the pan.)

3. Bake at 375° on an oven rack one-third up from bottom of oven 30 to 35 minutes or until a wooden pick inserted in center comes out clean. Invert cake onto a lightly greased (with shortening) wire rack; cool completely, with pan over cake (about 1 hour). Remove pan; peel foil off cake. Transfer cake to a serving platter. Spread Lemon-Cream Cheese Frosting evenly over top of cake.

Lemon-Cream Cheese Frosting

Beat 1½ (8-oz.) packages softened cream cheese and ¼ cup softened butter at medium speed with an electric mixer until creamy; add ¼ cup fresh lemon juice, beating just until blended. Gradually add 1 (16-oz.) package powdered sugar, beating at low speed until blended; stir in 2 tsp. lemon zest. Makes about 3½ cups.

Gumdrop Rose Petals

Using your thumbs and forefingers, flatten one small gumdrop to ⅛-inch thickness, lengthening and widening to form a petal shape. Dredge lightly in granulated sugar to prevent sticking as you work. Repeat procedure for desired number of petals. Place petals on a wire rack, and let stand uncovered for 24 hours.

INGREDIENTS

2½ cups sugar

1½ cups all-purpose flour

¼ tsp. table salt

2½ cups large egg whites

1 tsp. cream of tartar

1 tsp. vanilla extract

1 tsp. fresh lemon juice

Shortening

Lemon-Cream Cheese Frosting

Garnishes: Gumdrop Rose Petals, fresh mint leaves

INGREDIENTS

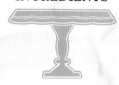

2 cups toasted slivered almonds

1½ cups sugar, divided

3 Tbsp. butter, melted

4 Tbsp. all-purpose flour, divided

Shortening

3 (8-oz.) packages cream cheese, softened

½ tsp. table salt

4 large eggs

1 (8-oz.) container sour cream

1 tsp. vanilla extract

1 Tbsp. lemon zest

1½ cups fresh blueberries

1 cup whipping cream

2 tsp. sugar

2 Tbsp. sour cream

Garnishes: blueberries, lemon rind curls

Blueberry Mini Cheesecakes

MAKES: 5 MINI CHEESECAKES · **HANDS-ON:** 30 MIN. · **TOTAL:** 10 HOURS, 43 MIN.

1. Preheat oven to 350°. Pulse almonds in a food processor 5 to 6 times or until finely ground. Combine ground almonds, ¼ cup sugar, 3 Tbsp. butter, and 1 Tbsp. flour in a small bowl. Press mixture onto bottom and halfway up sides of 5 lightly greased (with shortening) 4½-inch spring-form pans. Bake crusts at 350° for 8 minutes. Let cool on a wire rack. Reduce heat to 300°.

2. Beat cream cheese at medium speed with an electric mixer until smooth. Combine remaining 1¼ cups sugar, 3 Tbsp. flour, and ½ tsp. salt. Add to cream cheese, beating until blended. Add eggs, 1 at a time, beating well after each addition. Add 1 (8-oz.) container sour cream, vanilla, and lemon zest, beating just until blended. Gently stir in blueberries. Spoon about 1½ cups batter into each prepared crust. (Pans will be almost full. Batter will reach about ¼ inch from tops of pans.) Place on a baking sheet.

3. Bake at 300° for 35 to 40 minutes or until almost set. Turn oven off. Let cheesecakes stand in oven, with door partially open, 30 minutes. Remove cheesecakes from oven; gently run a knife around edges of cheesecakes to loosen. Cool in pans on a wire rack until completely cool (about 30 minutes). Cover and chill 8 hours. Remove sides of pans.

4. Beat whipping cream at high speed until foamy; gradually add 2 tsp. sugar, beating until stiff peaks form. Fold in 2 Tbsp. sour cream. Spread over cheesecakes.

NOTE: *To prepare cheesecakes using frozen blueberries, toss frozen berries with 2 Tbsp. all-purpose flour and 1 Tbsp. sugar. Proceed with recipe as directed.*

Blueberry Cheesecake: Prepare recipe as directed through Step 1, pressing mixture onto bottom and 1½ inches up sides of a lightly greased 9-inch springform pan. Proceed with recipe as directed through Step 2, pouring batter into prepared pan. Proceed with recipe as directed, increasing bake time to 1 hour and 10 minutes or until almost set.

Mini Red Velvet Cakes
with Mascarpone Frosting

MAKES: 6 MINI CAKES · HANDS-ON: 26 MIN. · TOTAL: 2 HOURS

Classic red velvet cake takes on a new twist as decadent mini desserts with a scattering of fresh raspberries.

1. Preheat oven to 350°. Stir together first 5 ingredients in a large bowl; make a well in center of mixture. Whisk together buttermilk and next 5 ingredients; add to flour mixture, stirring just until dry ingredients are moistened. Pour batter into a lightly greased (with shortening) and floured 13- x 9-inch pan.

2. Bake at 350° for 30 to 35 minutes or until a wooden pick inserted in center comes out clean. Cool in pan on a wire rack 10 minutes; remove from pan to wire rack, and cool completely (about 1 hour).

3. Cut cake into 6 rounds using a 3½-inch round cutter. Reserve remaining cake trimmings for another use. Split each mini cake in half horizontally. Spread about ⅓ cup Mascarpone Frosting between layers; spread remaining frosting on tops of cakes. Store cakes in refrigerator until ready to serve.

Mascarpone Frosting

Beat 1 (3-oz.) package softened cream cheese and ¼ cup softened butter at medium speed with an electric mixer until creamy; gradually add 5⅓ cups powdered sugar, beating at low speed until blended after each addition. Add 1 (8-oz.) package mascarpone cheese and 2 tsp. vanilla extract, beating until blended. Makes 3¾ cups.

INGREDIENTS

3½ cups all-purpose
soft-wheat flour

1¾ cups sugar

2 Tbsp. unsweetened cocoa

1½ tsp. baking soda

1¼ tsp. table salt

1⅓ cups buttermilk

1 cup vegetable oil

1 Tbsp. apple cider vinegar

2 tsp. vanilla extract

3 large eggs

1 (1-oz.) bottle red liquid
food coloring

Shortening

Mascarpone Frosting

Garnishes: fresh raspberries,
fresh mint leaves

PARTY
CAKES

Celebration Hummingbird Cake

MAKES: 12 SERVINGS • **HANDS-ON:** 30 MIN. • **TOTAL:** 8 HOURS, 40 MIN.

First printed in 1978, the Hummingbird Cake remains the most-requested *Southern Living* recipe of all time. The origin of the name is unknown, but its signature ingredients—mashed banana, pineapple, and pecans—assure its continued popularity.

1. Preheat oven to 350°. Stir together first 5 ingredients in a large bowl; stir in bananas and next 5 ingredients, stirring just until dry ingredients are moistened. Pour batter into 4 greased (with shortening) and floured 9-inch square or round cake pans.

2. Bake at 350° for 20 to 25 minutes or until a wooden pick inserted in center comes out clean. Cool in pans on wire racks 10 minutes; remove from pans to wire racks, and cool completely (about 1 hour).

3. Place 1 cake layer on a serving platter. Spoon about ½ cup Browned-Butter Frosting into a zip-top plastic bag. Snip 1 corner of bag to make a small hole. Pipe a ring of frosting around cake layer just inside the top edge. Top with Cream Cheese Custard Filling, and spread to edge of ring. Top with a second cake layer. Repeat procedure with frosting, filling, and next cake layer. Top with remaining cake layer, and spread frosting on top and sides of cake. Chill 1 hour before serving. Store in refrigerator.

Cream Cheese Custard Filling

Whisk together ¾ cup sugar and ⅓ cup all-purpose flour in a heavy saucepan; whisk in 3 large eggs and 1¼ cups milk until smooth. Cook over medium heat, whisking constantly, 8 to 10 minutes or until mixture reaches a chilled pudding-like thickness. Bring to a boil, whisking constantly; boil, whisking constantly, 1 minute. Remove from heat, and whisk in 1 (8-oz.) package cream cheese and 1 Tbsp. vanilla extract until cheese melts. Cool to room temperature (about 1 hour). Place plastic wrap directly on mixture (to prevent a film from forming), and chill 6 to 24 hours. Makes about 2⅔ cups.

INGREDIENTS

3 cups all-purpose flour

2 cups sugar

1 tsp. baking soda

1 tsp. table salt

1 tsp. ground cinnamon

2 cups diced ripe bananas (about 3 medium)

3 large eggs, beaten

1 cup chopped toasted pecans

1 cup vegetable oil

1 (8-oz.) can crushed pineapple, undrained

2 tsp. vanilla extract

Shortening

Browned-Butter Frosting (page 242)

Cream Cheese Custard Filling

INGREDIENTS

2 cups chopped walnuts

2½ cups self-rising flour

1½ tsp. ground cinnamon

1 tsp. baking soda

Shortening

Parchment paper

2 cups sugar

1 cup vegetable oil

4 large eggs

3 cups grated carrots

5-Cup Cream Cheese Frosting
(page 71)

Mama Dip's Carrot Cake

MAKES: 12 SERVINGS · **HANDS-ON:** 30 MIN. · **TOTAL:** 2 HOURS, 27 MIN.

This recipe from Chapel Hill, North Carolina, restaurateur Mildred "Mama Dip" Council makes one of the best carrot cakes we've tasted.

1. Preheat oven to 350°. Arrange walnuts in a single layer in a shallow pan. Bake 12 minutes or until toasted and fragrant.

2. Sift together flour, cinnamon, and baking soda. Line bottoms of 3 lightly greased (with shortening) 9-inch round cake pans with parchment paper; lightly grease parchment paper with shortening.

3. Beat sugar and oil at medium speed with an electric mixer until smooth. Add eggs, 1 at a time, beating until blended after each addition. Gradually add flour mixture, beating at low speed just until blended after each addition. Fold in carrots and 1 cup toasted walnuts. Spoon batter into prepared pans.

4. Bake at 350° for 35 to 40 minutes or until a wooden pick inserted in center comes out clean. Cool in pans on wire racks 10 minutes; remove from pans to wire racks. Carefully remove parchment paper, and discard; cool completely (about 1 hour).

5. Spread frosting between layers and on top and sides of cake; sprinkle remaining 1 cup toasted walnuts onto cake as desired.

Technique Tip

To make frosting this cake even easier, spread frosting between layers, and assemble cake. Refrigerate cake for 15 minutes before frosting sides and top of cake.

Carrot Cake
with Chèvre Frosting

MAKES: 8 SERVINGS • **HANDS-ON:** 40 MIN. • **TOTAL:** 2 HOURS, 35 MIN.

Substituting goat cheese for the standard cream cheese gives this frosting an extra-tangy kick.

1. Preheat oven to 350°. Grease (with shortening) 2 (8-inch) round cake pans; line bottoms with parchment paper, and grease (with shortening) and flour paper.

2. Stir together flour and next 3 ingredients.

3. Whisk together sugar and oil in a large bowl until well blended. Add eggs, 1 at a time, whisking until blended after each addition. Add flour mixture, stirring just until blended. Fold in carrots and next 3 ingredients. Spoon batter into prepared cake pans.

4. Bake at 350° for 40 to 45 minutes or until a wooden pick inserted in center comes out clean. Cool in pans on wire racks 15 minutes. Remove from pans to wire racks; carefully remove parchment paper, and discard. Cool completely (about 1 hour).

5. Spread ½ cup frosting between cake layers; spread remaining frosting on top and sides of cake.

Vanilla Chèvre Frosting

Beat 8 oz. goat cheese and ½ cup softened butter at medium speed with an electric mixer 2 to 3 minutes or until creamy. Add 1 (16-oz.) package powdered sugar, 1 cup at a time, beating at low speed until blended after each addition. Split 1 vanilla bean; scrape seeds into goat cheese mixture. Beat 30 seconds to 1 minute or until frosting is light and fluffy.

INGREDIENTS

Shortening

Parchment paper

2 cups all-purpose flour

2 tsp. baking soda

1 tsp. table salt

1 tsp. ground cinnamon

2 cups sugar

1¼ cups canola oil

3 large eggs

3 cups grated carrots

1 (8-oz.) can crushed pineapple
in juice, drained

1¼ cups coarsely chopped walnuts,
toasted

2 Tbsp. minced fresh ginger

Vanilla Chèvre Frosting

Garnishes: walnuts, carrot curls

INGREDIENTS

2⅓ cups finely chopped lightly toasted pecans, divided

Butter

2 cups all-purpose flour

2 tsp. baking soda

2 tsp. apple pie spice

½ tsp. table salt

3 large eggs, lightly beaten

2 cups sugar

¾ cup vegetable oil

¾ cup buttermilk

2 tsp. vanilla extract

2 cups peeled and grated Granny Smith apples

1½ cups grated carrots

⅔ cup plus 2 Tbsp. Apple Cider Caramel Sauce

Mascarpone Topping

Garnish: toasted pecan halves

Apple-Pecan Carrot Cake

MAKES: 10 SERVINGS · **HANDS-ON:** 30 MIN. · **TOTAL:** 3 HOURS, 30 MIN.

Top a showstopping crown of Mascarpone Topping with swirls of Apple Cider Caramel Sauce and a scattering of pecans. Caramel sauce, rather than frosting, sandwiches together the moist cake layers.

1. Preheat oven to 350°. Sprinkle 1⅓ cups toasted pecans into 2 well-buttered shiny 9-inch round cake pans; shake to coat bottom and sides of pans.

2. Stir together flour and next 3 ingredients.

3. Stir together eggs and next 4 ingredients in a large bowl until blended. Add flour mixture, stirring just until blended. Fold in apples, carrots, and remaining 1 cup pecans. Pour batter into prepared pans.

4. Bake at 350° for 30 to 35 minutes or until a wooden pick inserted in center comes out clean. Cool in pans on wire racks 10 minutes. Remove from pans to wire racks, and cool completely (about 1 hour).

5. Place 1 cake layer, pecan side down, on a serving plate. Spread top of cake layer with ⅔ cup Apple Cider Caramel Sauce; top with remaining cake layer, pecan side down. Spread Mascarpone Topping over top of cake. Drizzle 2 Tbsp. Apple Cider Caramel Sauce over topping, and swirl sauce into topping. Serve immediately.

Apple Cider Caramel Sauce

Cook 1 cup apple cider in a 3-qt. saucepan over medium heat, stirring often, 10 minutes or until reduced to ¼ cup. Stir in 1 cup firmly packed light brown sugar, ½ cup butter, and ¼ cup whipping cream. Bring to a boil over medium-high heat, stirring constantly; boil, stirring constantly, 2 minutes. Remove from heat, and cool completely. Makes about 1¼ cups.

Mascarpone Topping

Whisk together 1 (8-oz.) container mascarpone cheese, ¼ cup powdered sugar, and 2 tsp. vanilla extract in a large bowl just until blended. Beat 1 cup whipping cream at medium speed with an electric mixer until stiff peaks form. Gently fold into mascarpone mixture. Makes about 3 cups.

Red Velvet Cake

MAKES: 12 SERVINGS • **HANDS-ON:** 15 MIN. • **TOTAL:** 1 HOUR, 45 MIN.

1. Preheat oven to 350°. Beat butter at medium speed with an electric mixer until creamy. Gradually add sugar, beating until light and fluffy. Add eggs, 1 at a time, beating just until blended after each addition.

2. Combine flour, cocoa, and baking soda. Add to butter mixture alternately with sour cream, beginning and ending with flour mixture. Beat at low speed just until blended after each addition. Stir in vanilla; stir in red food coloring. Spoon cake batter into 3 greased (with shortening) and floured 8-inch round cake pans.

3. Bake at 350° for 18 to 20 minutes or until a wooden pick inserted in center comes out clean. Cool in pans on wire racks 10 minutes. Remove from pans to wire racks, and cool completely (about 1 hour).

4. Spread 5-Cup Cream Cheese Frosting between layers and on top and sides of cake.

5-Cup Cream Cheese Frosting

Beat 2 (8-oz.) packages softened cream cheese and ½ cup softened butter at medium speed with an electric mixer until creamy. Gradually add 2 (16-oz.) packages powdered sugar, beating until fluffy. Stir in 2 tsp. vanilla extract. Makes about 5 cups.

INGREDIENTS

1 cup butter, softened

2½ cups sugar

6 large eggs

3 cups all-purpose flour

3 Tbsp. unsweetened cocoa

¼ tsp. baking soda

1 (8-oz.) container sour cream

2 tsp. vanilla extract

2 (1-oz.) bottles red food coloring

Shortening

1½ recipes 5-Cup
Cream Cheese Frosting

3 large eggs

1 cup sugar

1 cup vegetable oil

½ cup buttermilk

1 tsp. vanilla extract

2 cups all-purpose flour

1 tsp. baking soda

1 tsp. table salt

1 tsp. ground cinnamon

½ tsp. ground cloves

½ tsp. ground nutmeg

½ cup fig preserves

½ cup applesauce

1 cup chopped toasted pecans

Shortening

Honey-Cream Cheese Frosting

Garnishes: dried figs,
fresh mint sprigs

Fig Cake

MAKES: 6 TO 8 SERVINGS • **HANDS-ON:** 20 MIN. • **TOTAL:** 2 HOURS, 13 MIN.

1. Preheat oven to 350°. Beat eggs, sugar, and oil at medium speed with an electric mixer until blended. Add buttermilk and vanilla; beat well.

2. Combine flour and next 5 ingredients; gradually add to buttermilk mixture, beating until blended. Fold in fig preserves, applesauce, and toasted pecans. (Batter will be thin.) Pour into 2 greased (with shortening) and floured 8-inch round cake pans.

3. Bake at 350° for 35 to 40 minutes or until a wooden pick inserted in center comes out clean. Cool in pans on wire racks 10 minutes. Remove from pans to wire racks, and cool completely (about 1 hour).

4. Spread Honey-Cream Cheese Frosting between layers and on top and sides of cake. Store cake in refrigerator.

NOTE: *We tested with Braswell's Fig Preserves.*

Honey-Cream Cheese Frosting

Beat 1½ (8-oz.) packages softened cream cheese, ⅓ cup softened butter, and 1½ Tbsp. honey at medium speed with an electric mixer just until smooth. Gradually add 2 cups sifted powdered sugar, beating at low speed just until blended. Makes 3½ cups.

Quick Bite

This recipe gets its figgy flavor from preserves. Buy them at the store or use homemade; if figs are in large pieces, coarsely chop them before adding to batter.

Caramel Cake

MAKES: 8 SERVINGS · **HANDS-ON:** 15 MIN. · **TOTAL:** 2 HOURS

This classic Caramel Frosting may seem daunting, but it is so worth the effort!

1. Preheat oven to 350°. Combine sour cream and milk.

2. Beat butter at medium speed with an electric mixer until creamy. Gradually add sugar, beating well. Add eggs, 1 at a time, beating until blended after each addition.

3. Combine flour, baking powder, and salt; add to butter mixture alternately with sour cream mixture, beginning and ending with flour mixture. Beat at medium-low speed until blended after each addition. Stir in vanilla. Pour batter into 2 greased (with shortening) and floured 9-inch round cake pans.

4. Bake at 350° for 30 to 35 minutes or until a wooden pick inserted in center comes out clean. Cool in pans on wire racks 10 minutes. Remove from pans to wire racks, and cool completely (about 1 hour).

5. Spread Classic Caramel Frosting between layers and on top and sides of cake.

Classic Caramel Frosting

Sprinkle ⅓ cup sugar in a shallow, heavy 3½-qt. Dutch oven; cook over medium heat, stirring constantly, 3 minutes or until sugar is melted and syrup is light golden brown (sugar will clump). Remove from heat. Stir together 1 Tbsp. flour and 2½ cups sugar in a large saucepan; add 1 cup milk, and bring to a boil over medium-high heat, stirring constantly. Gradually pour about one-fourth hot milk mixture into caramelized sugar, stirring constantly; gradually stir in remaining hot milk mixture until smooth. (Mixture will lump, but continue stirring until smooth.) Cover and cook over low heat 2 minutes. Increase heat to medium; uncover and cook, without stirring, until a candy thermometer reaches 238° (soft-ball stage, about 10 minutes). Add ¾ cup butter, stirring until blended. Remove from heat and let stand, without stirring, until temperature drops to 110° (about 1 hour). Pour into bowl of heavy-duty electric stand mixer. Add 1 tsp. vanilla, and beat at medium speed (setting 4) with whisk attachment until spreading consistency (about 20 minutes). Makes 3 cups.

INGREDIENTS

1 (8-oz.) container sour cream

¼ cup milk

1 cup butter, softened

2 cups sugar

4 large eggs

2¾ cups all-purpose flour

2 tsp. baking powder

½ tsp. table salt

1 tsp. vanilla extract

Shortening

Classic Caramel Frosting

INGREDIENTS

Vegetable cooking spray

Parchment paper

3½ cups all-purpose soft-wheat flour (such as White Lily)

2 tsp. baking powder

⅛ tsp. table salt

1 cup unsalted butter, softened

2 cups sugar, sifted

1 cup milk

1 tsp. vanilla extract

8 large egg whites

1 wooden skewer

Lane Cake Filling

Lane Cake

MAKES: 10 TO 12 SERVINGS · **HANDS-ON:** 50 MIN. · **TOTAL:** 7 HOURS, 30 MIN., INCLUDING FILLING

1. Preheat oven to 375°. Coat 2 (9-inch) round cake pans with cooking spray. Line bottom of each pan with parchment paper; coat paper with cooking spray. Sift together flour, baking powder, and salt 5 times, sifting from one bowl to another as you work.

2. Place butter and sugar in the bowl of a heavy-duty electric stand mixer, and beat at medium speed until light and fluffy. Add flour mixture to butter mixture alternately with milk, beginning and ending with flour mixture. Beat at low speed until blended after each addition. Add vanilla, and beat just until blended.

3. Beat egg whites with an electric mixer at high speed until stiff peaks form. Gently fold egg whites into batter. Divide batter between prepared pans.

4. Bake at 375° for 30 minutes or until lightly golden. Cool cake in pans 10 minutes. Remove from pans to wire racks, and cool completely (about 1 hour). Carefully remove parchment paper, and discard.

5. Place 1 cake layer on a cake stand or serving plate. Poke dozens of holes in top of cake using a wooden skewer, poking about halfway through cake and wiggling the skewer a little to widen the holes. Slowly pour half of filling over cake, letting the filling soak in. Top with remaining cake layer. Poke holes into top cake layer with skewer, poking all the way through and again wiggling the skewer to widen the holes. Pour remaining filling over top cake layer. (Filling will run over sides of cake.) Let stand 1 hour before serving. Store, covered, in refrigerator.

Lane Cake Filling

Combine 1 cup golden raisins and 1 cup dark rum. Cover and soak 4 to 24 hours. Place 8 egg yolks in a stainless-steel bowl, and beat at high speed with an electric mixer until fluffy. Add 1 cup sugar, and beat until very light yellow. Pour water to depth of 1 inch in a medium saucepan. Bring to a boil over high heat; reduce heat to low, and maintain at a simmer. Stir ½ cup butter into egg mixture; place bowl over pan of simmering water, and cook, stirring constantly, until a candy thermometer registers 160° (about 10 minutes). Remove from heat; stir in raisins and rum, 1½ cups unsweetened medium-to-large-flake coconut, 1 cup chopped toasted walnuts, and 1 tsp. vanilla. Makes 4¼ cups.

NOTE: *We tested with Bob's Red Mill Unsweetened Flaked Coconut.*

Italian Cream Cake

MAKES: 20 SERVINGS • **HANDS-ON:** 15 MIN. • **TOTAL:** 1 HOUR, 50 MIN.

1. Preheat oven to 350°. Beat butter and shortening in a large mixing bowl at medium speed with an electric mixer until creamy; gradually add sugar, beating well. Add egg yolks, 1 at a time, beating until blended after each addition. Add vanilla; beat just until blended.

2. Combine flour and baking soda; add to butter mixture alternately with buttermilk, beginning and ending with flour mixture. Beat at low speed just until blended after each addition. Stir in coconut.

3. Beat egg whites until stiff peaks form; fold into batter. Pour batter into 3 greased (with shortening) and floured 9-inch round cake pans.

4. Bake at 350° for 25 minutes or until a wooden pick inserted in center comes out clean. Cool in pans on wire racks 10 minutes. Remove from pans to wire racks, and cool completely (about 1 hour).

5. Spread Nutty Cream Cheese Frosting between layers and on top and sides of cake.

Nutty Cream Cheese Frosting

Beat 1 (8-oz.) package softened cream cheese, ½ cup softened butter, and 1 Tbsp. vanilla at medium speed with an electric mixer until creamy. Add 1 (16-oz.) package sifted powdered sugar, beating at low speed until blended. Beat frosting at high speed until smooth; stir in 1 cup chopped toasted pecans. Makes about 4 cups.

Serving Secret

Perfect for celebrations, this classic cake deserves a regal presentation. Place cake on a tall pedestal and arrange fresh fruit, pecan halves, and shaved coconut around the base or top edge.

INGREDIENTS

½ cup butter, softened

½ cup shortening

2 cups sugar

5 large eggs, separated

1 Tbsp. vanilla extract

2 cups all-purpose flour

1 tsp. baking soda

1 cup buttermilk

1 cup sweetened flaked coconut

Shortening

Nutty Cream Cheese Frosting

Garnish: toasted pecan halves

INGREDIENTS

½ cup butter, softened

½ cup shortening

1½ cups granulated sugar

½ cup firmly packed
dark brown sugar

5 large eggs, separated

1 Tbsp. vanilla extract

2 cups all-purpose flour

1 tsp. baking soda

1 cup buttermilk

1 cup finely chopped
toasted pecans

1 cup sweetened flaked coconut

Shortening

Quick Caramel Frosting

Cream Cheese Frosting (page 43)

3 cups toasted shaved coconut

Caramel Coconut Cream Cake

MAKES: 12 SERVINGS · **HANDS-ON:** 55 MIN. · **TOTAL:** 2 HOURS, 25 MIN.

Brown sugar is the shortcut to quick caramel flavor in both the cake layers and the frosting.

1. Preheat oven to 350°. Beat butter and shortening at medium speed with an electric mixer until fluffy; gradually add granulated and brown sugars, beating well. Add egg yolks, 1 at a time, beating until blended after each addition. Add vanilla, beating until blended.

2. Combine flour and baking soda; add to butter mixture alternately with buttermilk, beginning and ending with flour mixture. Beat at low speed just until blended after each addition. Stir in pecans and 1 cup sweetened flaked coconut.

3. Beat egg whites at high speed until stiff peaks form, and fold into batter. Pour batter into 3 greased (with shortening) and floured 9-inch round cake pans.

4. Bake at 350° for 23 to 25 minutes or until a wooden pick inserted in center comes out clean. Cool in pans on wire racks 10 minutes; remove from pans to wire racks, and cool completely (about 1 hour).

5. Prepare Quick Caramel Frosting. Immediately spread frosting between layers and on top of cake. Spread Cream Cheese Frosting over sides of cake; press toasted shaved coconut onto sides of cake.

Quick Caramel Frosting

Bring 1 cup butter, 1 cup firmly packed light brown sugar, and 1 cup firmly packed dark brown sugar to a rolling boil in a 3½-qt. saucepan over medium heat, whisking constantly (about 7 minutes). Stir in ½ cup heavy cream, and bring to a boil; remove from heat. Pour into bowl of a heavy-duty electric stand mixer. Gradually beat in 4 cups powdered sugar and 2 tsp. vanilla extract at medium speed, using whisk attachment; beat 8 to 12 minutes or until thickened. Use immediately. Makes 5 cups.

Ambrosia Cake

MAKES: 12 SERVINGS • **HANDS-ON:** 30 MIN. • **TOTAL:** 11 HOURS

1. Preheat oven to 350°. Beat butter at medium speed with a heavy-duty electric stand mixer until fluffy; gradually add sugar, beating well. Add egg yolks, 1 at a time, beating just until blended after each addition.

2. Combine flour and baking powder; stir together milk and coconut milk. Add flour mixture to butter mixture alternately with milk mixture, beginning and ending with flour mixture. Beat at low speed until blended after each addition. Stir in extracts.

3. Beat egg whites and salt at high speed until stiff peaks form. Stir about one-third egg whites into batter; fold in remaining egg whites. Spoon batter into 3 greased (with shortening) and floured 9-inch round cake pans.

4. Bake at 350° for 18 to 22 minutes or until a wooden pick inserted in center comes out clean. Cool in pans on wire racks 10 minutes; remove from pans to wire racks, and cool completely (about 1 hour).

5. Place 1 cake layer on a serving platter. Spoon ⅓ cup Vanilla Buttercream into a zip-top plastic bag. Snip 1 corner of bag to make a small hole. Pipe a ring of frosting around cake layer just inside the top edge. Top with half of Ambrosia Filling, and spread to edge of ring. Top with a second cake layer. Repeat procedure with frosting and filling. Top with remaining cake layer, and spread frosting on top and sides of cake.

Vanilla Buttercream

Beat 1 cup softened butter at medium speed with an electric mixer until creamy. Gradually add 1 tsp. vanilla extract and 1 cup powdered sugar. Gradually add 2¾ cups powdered sugar alternately with ¾ cup to 1 cup heavy cream, beating at low speed until blended after each addition. Stir in 1 tsp. vanilla extract. Beat at high speed until smooth. Makes 4½ cups.

Ambrosia Filling

Grate zest from 1 navel orange to equal 2 tsp. Peel and section orange; chop segments. Place orange and 1 (8-oz.) can crushed pineapple in a strainer, and drain. Whisk together ¾ cup sugar, 1 Tbsp. cornstarch, and ¼ tsp. table salt in a 3-qt. saucepan. Whisk in ¾ cup heavy cream and 3 large egg yolks. Bring to a boil over medium heat, whisking constantly; boil 1 minute or until thickened. Remove from heat; whisk in 2 Tbsp. butter and ¼ tsp. coconut extract. Stir in orange-pineapple mixture, 1 cup toasted sweetened coconut, and orange zest. Transfer to a bowl, place plastic wrap directly on filling, and chill 8 to 48 hours. Makes about 2¼ cups.

INGREDIENTS

1 cup butter, softened

2 cups sugar

4 large eggs, separated

3 cups all-purpose flour

1 Tbsp. baking powder

½ cup milk

½ cup coconut milk

1 tsp. vanilla extract

¼ tsp. coconut extract

⅛ tsp. table salt

Shortening

Vanilla Buttercream

Ambrosia Filling

Garnishes: toasted coconut shavings, maraschino cherries, edible flowers, candied orange slices, orange rind curls, fresh pineapple pieces

INGREDIENTS

½ cup butter, softened

2 cups sugar

5 large eggs, separated

2¼ cups all-purpose flour

1¼ tsp. baking soda

1 cup plus 2 Tbsp. buttermilk

1 tsp. almond extract

1 cup sweetened flaked coconut

1½ cups slivered toasted
almonds, divided

Shortening

5-Cup Cream Cheese Frosting
(page 71)

Toasted Almond Butter Cake

MAKES: 12 SERVINGS · **HANDS-ON:** 25 MIN. · **TOTAL:** 2 HOURS, 11 MIN.

1. Preheat oven to 350°. Beat butter at medium speed with an electric mixer until creamy. Gradually add sugar, beating well. Add egg yolks, 1 at a time, beating until blended after each addition.

2. Combine flour and baking soda; add to butter mixture alternately with buttermilk, beginning and ending with flour mixture. Beat at low speed just until blended after each addition. Stir in almond extract and coconut. Chop 1 cup almonds; add to batter.

3. Beat egg whites at high speed until stiff peaks form; fold into batter. Pour batter into 3 greased (with shortening) and floured 9-inch round cake pans.

4. Bake at 350° for 20 to 22 minutes or until a wooden pick inserted in center comes out clean. Cool in pans on wire racks 10 minutes. Remove from pans to wire racks, and cool completely (about 1 hour).

5. Spread 5-Cup Cream Cheese Frosting between layers and on top and sides of cake. Sprinkle with remaining ½ cup slivered almonds.

Technique Tip

This simple cake and smooth frosting are the perfect canvas for a beautiful frosted decoration. Look to page 9 for ideas and step-by-step instructions.

Luscious Lemon Cake

MAKES: 12 SERVINGS · **HANDS-ON:** 20 MIN. · **TOTAL:** 1 HOUR, 52 MIN.

1. Preheat oven to 375°. Beat egg yolks at high speed with an electric mixer 4 minutes or until thick and pale. Set aside.

2. Beat butter at medium speed until creamy; gradually add sugar, beating well. Add beaten egg yolks, beating well.

3. Combine flour, baking powder, and salt; add to butter mixture alternately with milk, beginning and ending with flour mixture. Beat at low speed just until blended after each addition. Stir in 1 tsp. lemon zest, 1 tsp. fresh lemon juice, and 1 tsp. vanilla. Spoon batter into 3 greased (with shortening) and floured 8-inch round cake pans.

4. Bake at 375° for 12 to 17 minutes or until a wooden pick inserted in center comes out clean. Cool in pans on wire racks 10 minutes. Remove from pans to wire racks, and cool completely (about 1 hour).

5. Spread Luscious Lemon Frosting between cake layers. Cover and chill until ready to serve.

Luscious Lemon Frosting

Beat 1 cup softened butter at medium speed with an electric mixer until creamy; stir in 2 tsp. lemon zest and ¼ cup fresh lemon juice. (Mixture will appear curdled.) Gradually add 2 (16-oz.) packages powdered sugar; beat at high speed 4 minutes or until spreading consistency. Gradually beat in up to 2 Tbsp. half-and-half, if necessary, for desired consistency. Makes 4 cups.

Serving Secret

For a more elegant presentation, make a double batch of the Luscious Lemon Frosting and frost the entire cake.

INGREDIENTS

8 large egg yolks

¾ cup butter, softened

1¼ cups sugar

2½ cups cake flour

1 Tbsp. baking powder

¼ tsp. table salt

¾ cup milk

1 tsp. lemon zest

1 tsp. fresh lemon juice

1 tsp. vanilla extract

Shortening

Luscious Lemon Frosting

1 cup butter, softened

2 cups sugar

4 large eggs, separated

3 cups all-purpose flour

1 Tbsp. baking powder

1 cup milk

1 tsp. vanilla extract

Shortening

Lemon Filling

Cream Cheese Frosting (page 43)

2 cups sweetened flaked coconut

Lemon-Coconut Cake

MAKES: 12 SERVINGS · **HANDS-ON:** 30 MIN. · **TOTAL:** 50 MIN.

This classic layer cake features a tangy lemon filling between layers of tender white cake and a rich coconut-cream cheese frosting.

1. Preheat oven to 350°. Beat butter at medium speed with an electric mixer until fluffy; gradually add sugar, beating well. Add egg yolks, 1 at a time, beating until blended after each addition.

2. Combine flour and baking powder; add to butter mixture alternately with milk, beginning and ending with flour mixture. Beat at low speed until blended after each addition. Stir in vanilla.

3. Beat egg whites at high speed with electric mixer until stiff peaks form; fold one-third of egg whites into batter. Gently fold in remaining beaten egg whites just until blended. Spoon batter into 3 greased (with shortening) and floured 9-inch round cake pans.

4. Bake at 350° for 18 to 20 minutes or until a wooden pick inserted in center comes out clean. Cool in pans on wire racks 10 minutes. Remove from pans to wire racks, and cool completely (about 1 hour).

5. Spread Lemon Filling between layers. Spread Cream Cheese Frosting on top and sides of cake. Sprinkle top and sides, if desired, with coconut.

Lemon Filling

Combine 1 cup sugar and ¼ cup cornstarch in a medium saucepan; whisk in 1 cup boiling water. Cook over medium heat, whisking constantly, until sugar and cornstarch dissolve (about 2 minutes). Gradually whisk about one-fourth of hot sugar mixture into 4 large lightly beaten egg yolks; add to remaining hot sugar mixture in pan, whisking constantly. Whisk in 2 tsp. lemon zest and ⅓ cup fresh lemon juice. Cook, whisking constantly, until mixture is thickened (about 2 to 3 minutes). Remove from heat. Whisk in 2 Tbsp. butter; let cool completely, stirring occasionally. Makes about 1⅔ cups.

Strawberry Mousse Cake

MAKES: 10 TO 12 SERVINGS • HANDS-ON: 45 MIN. • TOTAL: 5 HOURS, 15 MIN.

This beautiful cake is ideal for brunch, a baby shower, or any springtime celebration.

1. Preheat oven to 350°. Beat butter and sugar at medium speed with a heavy-duty electric stand mixer until fluffy. Gradually add egg whites, one-third at a time, beating well after each addition.

2. Sift together cake flour and baking powder; gradually add to butter mixture alternately with 1 cup water, beginning and ending with flour mixture. Stir in vanilla and almond extracts. Pour batter into 4 greased (with shortening) and floured 8-inch round cake pans.

3. Bake at 350° for 22 to 25 minutes or until a wooden pick inserted in center comes out clean. Cool in pans on wire racks 10 minutes. Remove from pans to wire racks, and cool completely (about 30 minutes).

4. Spread about 1 cup Strawberry Mousse between each cake layer, leaving a ¼-inch border around edges; cover and chill 3 hours or until mousse is set. Spread Fresh Strawberry Frosting on top and sides of cake.

Strawberry Mousse

Sprinkle 1 envelope unflavored gelatin over ¼ cup water in a small bowl; let stand 5 minutes. Process 2 cups sliced fresh strawberries and ¼ cup sugar in a blender or food processor until smooth, stopping to scrape down sides as needed. Transfer strawberry mixture to a small saucepan; bring to a boil over medium-high heat. Remove from heat. Add gelatin to strawberry mixture, stirring constantly until gelatin dissolves. Cover and chill until consistency of unbeaten egg whites, stirring occasionally (about 30 minutes). Beat 1 cup whipping cream at low speed until foamy; increase speed to medium-high, and beat until soft peaks form. Fold whipped cream into strawberry mixture until well blended. Cover and chill 30 minutes or just until mixture is thick enough to hold its shape when mounded. Makes about 3½ cups.

Fresh Strawberry Frosting

Beat ¾ cup softened butter at medium speed 20 seconds or until fluffy. Gradually add 5 cups powdered sugar and ¾ cup finely chopped fresh strawberries, beating at low speed until creamy. Makes about 4 cups.

INGREDIENTS

1¼ cups butter, softened

2¼ cups sugar

7 egg whites, at room temperature

3½ cups cake flour

4 tsp. baking powder

2 tsp. vanilla extract

½ tsp. almond extract

Shortening

Strawberry Mousse

Fresh Strawberry Frosting

Garnishes: halved fresh strawberries, edible flowers

2 cups sifted cake flour

2½ tsp. baking powder

½ tsp. table salt

1¼ cups sugar, divided

½ cup canola oil

¼ cup fresh lemon juice

4 large egg yolks

8 large egg whites

1 tsp. cream of tartar

Shortening

Strawberry Jam Filling

Strawberries-and-Cream Frosting

Garnishes: fresh mint leaves,
edible flowers

Strawberries-and-Cream Cake

MAKES: 12 SERVINGS · **HANDS-ON:** 30 MIN. · **TOTAL:** 10 HOURS, 22 MIN.

1. Preheat oven to 350°. Stir together first 3 ingredients and 1 cup sugar in a large bowl. Make a well in center of mixture; add oil, next 2 ingredients, and ¼ cup water. Beat at medium-high speed with an electric mixer 3 to 4 minutes or until smooth.

2. Beat egg whites and cream of tartar at medium-high speed until soft peaks form. Gradually add remaining ¼ cup sugar, 1 Tbsp. at a time, beating until stiff peaks form. Gently stir one-fourth of egg white mixture into flour mixture; gently fold in remaining egg white mixture. Spoon batter into 6 greased (with shortening) and floured 8-inch round cake pans.

3. Bake at 350° for 12 to 15 minutes or until a wooden pick inserted in center comes out clean. Cool in pans on wire racks 10 minutes; remove from pans to wire racks, and cool completely (about 1 hour).

4. Spread Strawberry Jam Filling between cake layers, leaving a ¼-inch border around edges (about ⅔ cup between each layer). Cover cake with plastic wrap, and chill 8 to 24 hours. Spread Strawberries-and-Cream Frosting on top and sides of cake. Chill 2 hours before serving.

Strawberry Jam Filling

Stir together 4 cups mashed fresh strawberries and 2½ cups sugar in a large saucepan; let stand 30 minutes. Bring strawberry mixture to a boil over medium heat; boil 5 minutes. Remove from heat, and stir in 1 (3-oz.) package strawberry-flavored gelatin until dissolved; cool completely (about 1 hour). Cover and chill 8 hours. Makes about 4 cups.

Strawberries-and-Cream Frosting

Stir together 1 Tbsp. strawberry-flavored gelatin and 2 Tbsp. boiling water in a small bowl; cool completely (about 20 minutes). Beat 1 cup whipping cream and gelatin mixture at high speed with an electric mixer until foamy; gradually add ¼ cup sugar, beating until soft peaks form. Stir in 1 (8-oz.) container sour cream, ¼ cup at a time, stirring just until blended after each addition. Makes about 3½ cups.

Strawberry Birthday Cake

MAKES: 16 SERVINGS • **HANDS-ON:** 53 MIN. • **TOTAL:** 2 HOURS, 46 MIN.

1. Preheat oven to 350°. Beat butter at medium speed with an electric mixer until creamy; gradually add sugar, beating well. Add eggs, 1 at a time, beating until blended after each addition.

2. Combine flour, baking powder, and salt; add to butter mixture alternately with milk, beginning and ending with flour mixture. Beat at low speed until blended after each addition, stopping to scrape bowl as needed. Split vanilla bean lengthwise, and scrape out seeds. Stir seeds into batter; reserve bean for another use. Pour batter into 2 greased (with shortening) and floured 8-inch round cake pans with 2-inch sides.

3. Bake at 350° for 30 to 34 minutes or until a wooden pick inserted in center comes out clean. Cool in pans on wire racks 10 minutes; remove from pans to wire racks, and cool completely (about 1 hour).

4. Using a serrated knife, slice cake layers in half horizontally to make 4 layers. Place 1 layer, cut side up, on a cake plate or serving platter. Spread with half of Strawberry Compote. Top with another cake layer; spread with about ¾ cup Cream Cheese Frosting. Place another cake layer on top of frosting; spread with remaining compote. Top with remaining cake layer. Spread 1¼ cups frosting on top and sides of cake to create a thin coat of frosting. Chill cake 30 minutes. Spread top and sides of cake with remaining frosting. Store in refrigerator.

Strawberry Compote

Split 1 vanilla bean lengthwise, and scrape out seeds. Stir together vanilla bean and seeds, 1½ cups chopped fresh strawberries, and ½ cup sugar in a medium saucepan. Cook over medium heat, stirring occasionally, 10 minutes or until strawberries are soft and mixture is slightly syrupy. Remove from heat; discard vanilla bean. Stir in 1 Tbsp. rum. Cool completely (about 30 min).

INGREDIENTS

1 cup butter, softened

2 cups sugar

3 large eggs

2¾ cups all-purpose soft-wheat flour

2 tsp. baking powder

½ tsp. table salt

1 cup milk

1 vanilla bean

Shortening

Strawberry Compote

5-Cup Cream Cheese Frosting (page 71)

Garnish: fresh strawberry halves

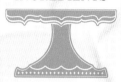

Shortening

3 oz. unsweetened baking chocolate, chopped

½ cup butter

1 cup hot water

2 cups all-purpose flour

2 cups packed brown sugar

1½ tsp. baking soda

½ tsp. table salt

2 large eggs

½ cup sour cream

1 tsp. vanilla extract

⅓ cup granulated sugar

⅓ cup coffee-flavored liqueur

White Chocolate Whipped Cream

Black-and-White Chocolate Torte

MAKES: 12 SERVINGS · **HANDS-ON:** 45 MIN. · **TOTAL:** 2 HOURS, 45 MIN.

1. Preheat oven to 350°. Grease bottoms only of 2 (8- or 9-inch) round cake pans with shortening; lightly flour.

2. Cook chocolate, butter, and 1 cup hot water in a 2-qt. saucepan over medium heat, stirring occasionally, until melted and smooth. Remove from heat; cool 5 minutes. Mix flour, brown sugar, baking soda, and salt in a large bowl. Add melted chocolate mixture, beating at medium speed just until blended. Add eggs, 1 at a time, beating until blended. Beat in sour cream and vanilla. Pour batter into prepared pans.

3. Bake at 350° for 30 to 32 minutes or until a wooden pick inserted in center comes out clean. Cool in pans on wire racks 10 minutes. Remove from pans to wire racks, and cool completely (about 1 hour).

4. Meanwhile, mix granulated sugar, liqueur, and 1 Tbsp. water in a 1-qt. saucepan. Heat to boiling, stirring occasionally, until sugar is dissolved; remove from heat. Cool completely.

5. Using a serrated knife, slice cake layers in half horizontally to make 4 layers. Brush about 2 Tbsp. liqueur mixture over cut side of each layer; let stand 1 minute.

6. Place 1 cake layer, cut side up, on serving plate; spread with 1 cup White Chocolate Whipped Cream to within ¼ inch of edge. Top with another layer, cut side down; spread with 1 cup whipped cream mixture. Repeat with remaining layers. Spread top and sides of cake with remaining whipped cream mixture. Store loosely covered in refrigerator.

White Chocolate Whipped Cream

Microwave ½ cup whipping cream and 12 oz. white chocolate baking bars in a glass bowl at HIGH 45 to 60 seconds or until mixture can be stirred smooth with whisk. Cover surface directly with plastic wrap to prevent a film from forming; refrigerate 30 minutes or until cooled but not firm. Beat white chocolate mixture and 3 cups whipping cream in a large bowl at medium speed with an electric mixer until soft peaks form. Makes 5 cups.

Chocolate Turtle Cake

MAKES: 16 SERVINGS · **HANDS-ON:** 40 MIN. · **TOTAL:** 4 HOURS, 25 MIN.

1. Preheat oven to 350°. Grease 2 (9-inch) round cake pans with shortening; sprinkle with cocoa.

2. Beat cake mix and next 6 ingredients at low speed with an electric mixer for 1 minute. Beat at medium speed 2 minutes. Fold in chocolate morsels and chopped pecans. Pour batter into prepared pans.

3. Bake at 350° for 30 to 32 minutes or until a wooden pick inserted in center comes out clean. Cool in pans on wire racks 10 minutes. Remove from pans to wire racks, and cool completely (about 1 hour). Wrap cake layers in plastic wrap; refrigerate at least 1 hour.

4. Stir frosting and dulce de leche in a medium bowl with a whisk until well blended; set aside. Cut 6 turtle candies in half; set aside for garnish. Chop remaining candies.

5. Place 1 cake layer, top side up, on serving plate. Spread with half of frosting mixture; sprinkle with chopped candies. Place second cake layer, top side up, on candies. Spread remaining frosting mixture on top of cake. Cover; refrigerate until serving time. Drizzle caramel topping over top of cake, allowing some to drip down side. Top cake with pecan halves and reserved turtle candies.

Serving Secret

With exposed chocolate layers, piles of frosting, and pieces of turtle candies and pecans to adorn the top, this cake is a showstopper. Hold back on the caramel drizzle for the prettiest look, and serve extra on the side.

INGREDIENTS

Shortening

Unsweetened cocoa

1 (18.25-oz.) package devil's food cake mix

1 (3.9-oz.) package chocolate instant pudding mix

3 large eggs

1¼ cups milk

1 cup canola oil

1 Tbsp. vanilla extract

1 tsp. instant coffee granules

1 (6-oz.) package semisweet chocolate morsels

1 cup chopped pecans

1 (16-oz.) container ready-to-spread cream cheese frosting

½ cup canned dulce de leche

2 (7-oz.) packages turtle candies

1 (12-oz.) jar caramel ice-cream topping

¼ cup pecan halves, toasted

INGREDIENTS

9 fun-size or 21 mini
chocolate-coated caramel
and creamy nougat bars

½ cup butter

2 cups sugar

1 cup shortening

3 large eggs

2½ cups all-purpose flour

1 tsp. table salt

1½ cups buttermilk

½ tsp. baking soda

1 tsp. vanilla extract

Shortening

Chocolate-Marshmallow Frosting

Garnish: chopped frozen fun-size
chocolate-coated caramel
and creamy nougat bars

Heavenly Candy Bar Cake

MAKES: 12 SERVINGS · **HANDS-ON:** 15 MIN. · **TOTAL:** 50 MIN.

Gooey chunks of candy bar really do take this cake to realms above. Melted candy bars are stirred into the batter, while frozen bars are coarsely chopped and pressed around the sides of the cake.

1. Preheat oven to 350°. Melt candy bars and butter in a heavy saucepan over low heat about 5 minutes, stirring until smooth. Set aside.

2. Beat sugar and 1 cup shortening at medium speed with an electric mixer about 3 minutes or until well blended. Add eggs, 1 at a time, beating just until blended after each addition.

3. Combine flour and salt. Stir together buttermilk and baking soda. Gradually add flour mixture to sugar mixture, alternately with buttermilk mixture, beginning and ending with flour mixture. Beat at low speed just until blended after each addition. Stir in melted candy bar mixture and vanilla. Spoon batter into 3 greased (with shortening) and floured 9-inch round cake pans.

4. Bake at 350° for 30 minutes or until a wooden pick inserted in center comes out clean. Cool in pans on wire racks 10 minutes. Remove from pans to wire racks, and cool completely (about 1 hour). Spread half of Chocolate-Marshmallow Frosting evenly between cake layers. Spread remaining frosting evenly over top and sides of cake.

NOTE: *We tested with Milky Way bars.*

Chocolate-Marshmallow Frosting

Melt 3 cups miniature marshmallows, ¾ cup butter, ¾ cup evaporated milk, and 6 oz. chopped unsweetened chocolate baking squares in a 2-qt. saucepan over medium-low heat, stirring 5 minutes or until mixture is smooth. Transfer chocolate mixture to a large bowl. Place bowl into a larger bowl filled with ice and water. Gradually add 6 cups powdered sugar, beating at low speed with an electric mixer. Increase speed to medium-high, and beat 5 minutes or until frosting is cool, thick, and spreadable. Stir in 1 Tbsp. vanilla extract. Makes 4½ cups.

Blackberry-Chocolate Spice Cake

MAKES: 12 SERVINGS • **HANDS-ON:** 35 MIN. • **TOTAL:** 2 HOURS, 17 MIN.

Chocolate and spices mingle with sweet blackberries under a robe of chocolate fudge frosting drizzled with blackberry sauce. Even grandmothers would be pleased with this updated classic.

1. Preheat oven to 350°. Grease 2 (9-inch) round cake pans with shortening, and dust with cocoa. Set aside.

2. Beat cake mix and next 11 ingredients at low speed with an electric mixer 1 minute; beat at medium speed 2 minutes. Fold in chopped chocolate. Pour batter into prepared pans.

3. Bake at 350° for 30 to 32 minutes or until a wooden pick inserted in center comes out clean. Cool in pans on a wire racks 10 minutes. Remove from pans to wire racks, and cool completely (about 1 hour). Wrap cake layers in plastic wrap and chill at least 1 hour or up to 24 hours.

4. Using a serrated knife, slice cake layers in half horizontally to make 4 layers. Place 1 layer, cut side up, on cake plate. Spread one-fourth of blackberry pie filling over cake. Repeat procedure twice. Place final cake layer on top of cake, cut side down. Spread chocolate fudge frosting on top and sides of cake. Drizzle remaining filling over top of cake, letting it drip down sides of cake. Cover and chill in refrigerator until ready to serve.

NOTE: *We tested with Green & Black's Organic candy bar.*

INGREDIENTS

Shortening

Unsweetened cocoa

1 (18.25-oz.) package devil's food cake mix

1 (3.4-oz.) package chocolate instant pudding mix

3 large eggs

1¼ cups milk

1 cup canola oil

1 Tbsp. vanilla extract

1 tsp. chocolate extract

½ tsp. almond extract

2 tsp. ground cinnamon

¼ tsp. ground ginger

¼ tsp. ground nutmeg

¼ tsp. ground cloves

2 (3.5-oz.) bittersweet dark chocolate with orange and spices candy bars, chopped

1 (21-oz.) can blackberry pie filling

2 (16-oz.) containers chocolate fudge frosting

Garnish: fresh blackberries

INGREDIENTS

Parchment paper

Masking tape

1 cup chopped toasted pecans

2 Tbsp. cornstarch

⅛ tsp. table salt

2 cups sugar, divided

7 egg whites, at room temperature

½ tsp. cream of tartar

2 (8-oz.) containers
mascarpone cheese

2 tsp. vanilla extract

3 cups whipping cream

4½ cups sliced fresh strawberries

Halved fresh strawberries

Fresh Strawberry Meringue Cake

MAKES: 10 TO 12 SERVINGS · **HANDS-ON:** 1 HOUR · **TOTAL:** 4 HOURS, 20 MIN.

Serve this dessert in the springtime when strawberries are at their ripe, juicy peak.

1. Preheat oven to 250°. Cover 2 large baking sheets with parchment paper. Draw 2 (8-inch) circles on each sheet of parchment by tracing an 8-inch round cake pan. Turn paper over; secure with masking tape.

2. Process pecans, cornstarch, salt, and ½ cup sugar in a food processor 40 to 45 seconds or until pecans are finely ground.

3. Beat egg whites and cream of tartar at high speed with an electric mixer until foamy. Gradually add 1 cup sugar, 1 Tbsp. at a time, beating at medium-high speed until mixture is glossy, stiff peaks form, and sugar dissolves (2 to 4 minutes; do not overbeat). Add half of pecan mixture to egg white mixture, gently folding just until blended. Repeat procedure with remaining pecan mixture. Gently spoon egg white mixture onto circles drawn on parchment paper (about 1½ cups mixture per circle), spreading to cover each circle completely.

4. Bake at 250° for 1 hour, turning baking sheets after 30 minutes. Turn oven off; let meringues stand in closed oven with light on 2 to 2½ hours.

5. Just before assembling cake, stir together mascarpone cheese and vanilla in a large bowl just until blended. Beat whipping cream at low speed until foamy; increase speed to medium-high, and gradually add remaining ½ cup sugar, beating until stiff peaks form. (Do not overbeat or cream will be grainy.) Gently fold whipped cream into mascarpone mixture.

6. Carefully remove 1 meringue from parchment paper; place on a cake plate or serving platter. Spread one-fourth mascarpone mixture (about 2 cups) over meringue; top with 1½ cups sliced strawberries. Repeat layers 2 times; top with remaining meringue, mascarpone mixture, and halved strawberries. Serve immediately, or chill up to 2 hours. Cut with a sharp, thin-bladed knife.

Mocha-Hazelnut Dacquoise

MAKES: 10 TO 12 SERVINGS • **HANDS-ON:** 33 MIN. • **TOTAL:** 3 HOURS, 48 MIN., PLUS 1 DAY FOR CHILLING

1. Preheat oven to 275°. Line 2 large baking sheets with parchment paper. Draw 2 (8-inch) circles on each sheet of parchment by tracing an 8-inch round cake pan. Turn parchment paper over; secure with masking tape.

2. Process 1 cup hazelnuts, powdered sugar, and cornstarch in a food processor until hazelnuts are finely ground.

3. Beat egg whites and cream of tartar at high speed with an electric mixer until foamy. Gradually add granulated sugar, 1 Tbsp. at a time, beating until stiff peaks form and sugar dissolves (about 2 to 4 minutes). Gently fold in ground hazelnut mixture in 4 additions.

4. Spoon one-fourth meringue batter into center of each circle on parchment paper-lined baking sheets. Spread evenly to edges of each circle using a small offset spatula.

5. Bake at 275° for 1 hour and 15 minutes or until crisp and lightly golden. Turn off oven; let meringues stand in closed oven 1 hour. Remove from oven; cool completely on baking sheets on wire racks (about 30 minutes). Carefully peel off parchment paper.

6. Place 1 meringue on a serving plate. Top with one-fourth Mocha Cream Filling, spreading almost to edges of meringue. Repeat layers twice. Top with remaining meringue layer. Spread remaining filling on top of meringue. Sprinkle with remaining ¼ cup chopped hazelnuts and chocolate shavings. Cover and chill 8 to 24 hours before serving.

Mocha Cream Filling

Place 2 (4-oz.) chopped chocolate baking bars in a large bowl. Bring ¾ cup heavy cream to a simmer in a small saucepan over medium-high heat. Pour cream over chocolate; let stand 1 minute. Whisk until chocolate is melted and smooth. Cool to room temperature (about 30 minutes). Beat chocolate mixture, 2¼ cups heavy cream, ¼ cup powdered sugar, 2 Tbsp. coffee liqueur, and 1 Tbsp. instant espresso at high speed with an electric mixer until stiff peaks form. Makes 5 cups.

INGREDIENTS

Parchment paper

Masking tape

1¼ cups coarsely chopped toasted hazelnuts

¾ cup powdered sugar

1 Tbsp. cornstarch

6 large egg whites

½ tsp. cream of tartar

¾ cup granulated sugar

Mocha Cream Filling

Chocolate shavings

¾ cup granulated sugar

¼ cup cornstarch

⅛ tsp. kosher salt

4 large egg yolks

2 cups half-and-half

3 Tbsp. butter

2 Tbsp. Key lime zest*

½ cup fresh Key lime juice*

45 graham cracker squares

1 cup whipping cream

¼ cup powdered sugar

Garnishes: lime slices, mint leaves

Key Lime Icebox Cake

MAKES: 8 TO 10 SERVINGS · **HANDS-ON:** 40 MIN. · **TOTAL:** 9 HOURS, 40 MIN.

This refreshing summertime cake is really a super-sneaky shortcut in cake baking—there's no cake to bake! Instead, graham crackers sandwich a tart custard.

1. Whisk together first 3 ingredients in a heavy saucepan. Whisk together egg yolks and half-and-half in a bowl. Gradually whisk egg mixture into sugar mixture; bring to a boil over medium heat, whisking constantly. Boil, whisking constantly, 1 minute; remove from heat. Whisk in butter and zest until butter melts. Gradually whisk in juice just until blended. Pour into a metal bowl, and place bowl on ice. Let stand, stirring occasionally, 8 to 10 minutes or until custard is cold and slightly thickened.

2. Meanwhile, line bottom and sides of an 8-inch square pan with plastic wrap, allowing 4 inches to extend over sides. Place 9 graham crackers, with sides touching, in a single layer in bottom of pan to form a large square. (Crackers will not completely cover bottom.)

3. Spoon about ¾ cup cold custard over crackers; spread to edge of crackers. Repeat layers 3 times with crackers and remaining custard, ending with custard; top with remaining 9 crackers. Pull sides of plastic wrap tightly over cake; freeze in pan 8 hours. Lift cake from pan, and place on a platter; discard plastic wrap. Cover loosely; let stand 1 hour.

4. Beat whipping cream at high speed with an electric mixer until foamy; gradually add powdered sugar, beating until soft peaks form. Spread on top of cake.

Regular (Persian) lime zest and juice may be substituted.

Technique Tip

Add the lime juice after you've fully cooked the custard in order to let the cornstarch thicken the mixture properly.

Gingerbread Cake
with Stout Buttercream

MAKES: 12 SERVINGS · **HANDS-ON:** 15 MIN. · **TOTAL:** 2 HOURS

1. Preheat oven to 350°. Stir together gingerbread cake mix, eggs, and 2½ cups stout beer in a large bowl until combined. Pour batter evenly into 2 lightly greased (with shortening) 8-inch square pans.

2. Bake at 350° for 35 minutes or until a wooden pick inserted in center comes out clean. Cool in pans on wire racks 10 minutes. Remove from pans to wire racks, and cool completely (about 1 hour).

3. Beat softened butter at medium speed with an electric mixer until creamy. Gradually add powdered sugar and remaining ¼ cup stout beer, beating until blended after each addition. Beat 1 minute or until light and fluffy.

4. Spread stout buttercream between layers and on top of cake.

NOTE: *We tested with Betty Crocker Gingerbread Cake & Cookie Mix. We used Terrapin Wake-n-Bake Coffee Oatmeal Imperial Stout at one testing and Guinness Extra Stout beer at another.*

Serving Secret

With its square shape and exposed gingerbread layers, this cake is a standout at any feast. Serve cake surrounded by fresh rosemary sprigs, and serve slices along with a rich stout beer.

INGREDIENTS

2 (14.5-oz.) packages
gingerbread cake mix

2 large eggs

2¾ cups stout beer, at room
temperature, divided
(about 2 [12-oz.] bottles)

Shortening

½ cup butter, softened

1 (16-oz.) package powdered sugar

Garnishes: toasted pecans,
rosemary sprigs

INGREDIENTS

½ cup butter, softened

½ cup shortening

2 cups sugar

3 cups cake flour

4 tsp. baking powder

½ tsp. table salt

⅔ cup milk

2 tsp. vanilla extract

¾ tsp. almond extract

6 large egg whites

Shortening

Milk Chocolate Frosting

Garnish: multicolored candy sprinkles

Birthday Cake

MAKES: 12 SERVINGS · **HANDS-ON:** 15 MIN. · **TOTAL:** 7 HOURS, 5 MIN.

This recipe bakes up into a tender three-layer white cake. (Freezing the layers before frosting them makes assembly easy.) It's an ideal birthday cake for young ones, picky eaters, and purists!

1. Preheat oven to 325°. Beat butter and shortening at medium speed with an electric mixer until creamy; gradually add sugar, beating well.

2. Combine flour, baking powder, and salt; add to butter mixture alternately with milk and ⅔ cup water, beginning and ending with flour mixture. Beat at low speed until blended after each addition. Stir in extracts.

3. Beat egg whites at high speed with electric mixer until stiff peaks form; fold about one-third of egg whites into batter. Gradually fold in remaining egg whites. Pour cake batter into 3 greased (with shortening) and floured 8-inch round cake pans.

4. Bake at 325° for 25 to 30 minutes or until a wooden pick inserted in center comes out clean. Cool in pans on wire racks 10 minutes. Remove from pans to wire racks, and cool completely (about 1 hour). Wrap each layer in plastic wrap. Freeze 4 hours.

5. Unwrap frozen cake layers. Spread Milk Chocolate Frosting between layers and on top and sides of cake. Let stand at room temperature 2 hours before serving.

Milk Chocolate Frosting

Beat 1 cup softened butter at medium speed with an electric mixer until creamy. Add 6 cups powdered sugar, ⅓ cup unsweetened cocoa, and ½ cup milk, beating until smooth. Makes 4 cups.

Tiramisù Layer Cake

MAKES: 10 TO 12 SERVINGS • **HANDS-ON:** 45 MIN. • **TOTAL:** 6 HOURS, 40 MIN.

This cake combines the flavor of traditional tiramisù with a layer cake that you can decorate.

1. Preheat oven to 350°. Beat butter and ½ cup shortening at medium speed with an electric mixer until fluffy; gradually add sugar, beating well.

2. Stir together milk and ⅔ cup water. Combine flour and next 2 ingredients; add to butter mixture alternately with milk mixture, beginning and ending with flour mixture. Beat at low speed just until blended after each addition. Stir in vanilla bean paste and almond extract.

3. Beat egg whites at high speed until stiff peaks form, and fold into batter. Spoon batter into 3 greased (with shortening) and floured 8-inch round cake pans.

4. Bake at 350° for 25 to 30 minutes or until a wooden pick inserted in center comes out clean. Cool in pans on wire racks 10 minutes; remove from pans to wire racks, and cool completely (about 1 hour).

5. Pierce cake layers with a wooden pick, making holes 1 inch apart. Brush or spoon Coffee Syrup over layers.

6. Place 1 cake layer, brushed side up, on a cake stand or serving plate. Spread top with 1⅓ cups Mascarpone Frosting. Top with second cake layer, brushed side up, and spread with 1⅓ cups frosting. Top with remaining cake layer, brushed side up. Spread top and sides of cake with remaining frosting. Chill 4 hours before serving.

*Vanilla extract may be substituted for vanilla bean paste.

Coffee Syrup

Combine 1 cup sugar and ⅓ cup water in a microwave-safe bowl. Microwave at HIGH 1½ minutes or until sugar is dissolved, stirring at 30-second intervals. Stir in ⅔ cup strong brewed coffee and ¼ cup brandy. Let cool 1 hour. Makes about 1½ cups.

INGREDIENTS

½ cup butter, softened

½ cup shortening

2 cups sugar

⅔ cup milk

3 cups all-purpose flour

1 Tbsp. baking powder

1 tsp. table salt

1 Tbsp. vanilla bean paste*

1 tsp. almond extract

6 large egg whites

Shortening

Coffee Syrup

2 recipes
Mascarpone Frosting
(page 59)

Garnishes: raspberries, strawberries, red currants, fresh mint

SUNDAY AFTERNOON
CAKES

White Chocolate-Cranberry Cheesecake

MAKES: 6 TO 8 SERVINGS · **HANDS-ON:** 35 MIN. · **TOTAL:** 12 HOURS, 40 MIN.

1. Preheat oven to 350°. Pulse wafer cookies and chopped semisweet chocolate in a food processor 8 to 10 times or until mixture resembles fine crumbs. Stir together crumb mixture, melted butter, and ¼ cup sugar; firmly press on bottom, up sides, and onto lip of a lightly greased (with shortening) 10-inch pie plate. Bake at 350° for 10 minutes. Transfer to a wire rack, and cool completely (about 30 minutes). Reduce oven temperature to 325°.

2. Microwave white chocolate and whipping cream at MEDIUM (50% power) 1 to 1½ minutes or until melted and smooth, stirring at 30-second intervals.

3. Beat cream cheese, flour, and ⅓ cup sugar at medium speed with an electric mixer 1 minute or until creamy and smooth. Add eggs, 1 at a time, beating just until blended after each addition. Add cranberries, next 2 ingredients, and white chocolate mixture. Beat at low speed just until blended. Spoon batter into prepared crust.

4. Bake at 325° for 30 to 35 minutes or until set. Cool completely on a wire rack (about 2 hours). Cover and chill 8 hours. Spoon Cranberry Topping over pie before serving.

Cranberry Topping

Bring 1 (12-oz.) package fresh cranberries, 1 cup sugar, and ¼ cup water to a boil in a 3-qt. saucepan over medium-high heat, stirring often. Boil, stirring often, 6 to 8 minutes or until mixture thickens to a syrup-like consistency. Remove from heat, and stir in ½ cup seedless raspberry jam. Cool completely (about 1 hour). Cover and chill 8 hours. Makes 2½ cups.

INGREDIENTS

1 (9-oz.) package chocolate wafer cookies

½ (4-oz.) semisweet chocolate baking bar, chopped

½ cup butter, melted

¼ cup sugar

Shortening

1 (6-oz.) package white chocolate baking bars, chopped

¼ cup whipping cream

2 (8-oz.) packages cream cheese, softened

2 Tbsp. all-purpose flour

⅓ cup sugar

4 large eggs

½ cup chopped sweetened dried cranberries

½ (4-oz.) semisweet chocolate baking bar, finely chopped

¼ cup amaretto liqueur

Cranberry Topping

Garnish: fresh mint leaves

INGREDIENTS

1½ cups walnut halves

1 cup sugar, divided

2 Tbsp. unsalted butter, melted

Shortening

2½ (8-oz.) packages
cream cheese, softened

1 (8-oz.) package
mascarpone cheese, softened

3 large eggs

1 tsp. almond extract

¼ tsp. table salt

5 (3-oz.) pieces baklava

12 walnut halves

Honey Syrup

Baklava Cheesecake

MAKES: 10 SERVINGS · **HANDS-ON:** 18 MIN. · **TOTAL:** 11 HOURS, 50 MIN.

Purchase prepared baklava from a local Greek restaurant, or, if you have time, make your own. It's the hidden surprise in each slice of this decadent dessert.

1. Preheat oven to 350°. Pulse 1½ cups walnuts and ¼ cup sugar in a food processor 4 or 5 times or until walnuts are finely ground. Add butter; pulse until mixture resembles coarse sand. Press mixture firmly on bottom of a lightly greased (with shortening) 9-inch springform pan. Bake 12 to 14 minutes or until lightly browned. Cool on a wire rack.

2. Reduce oven temperature to 300°. Beat cream cheese, mascarpone, and remaining ¾ cup sugar at medium speed with an electric mixer until blended. Add eggs, 1 at a time, beating just until blended after each addition. Add almond extract and salt, beating at low speed just until blended.

3. Cut each baklava piece into 2 small triangles, about 2 x 3 inches. Arrange baklava pieces in a ring over baked crust, with pointed end of each piece pointing toward center and wide ends around outside edge of pan. Pour batter over baklava into baked crust.

4. Bake at 300° for 1 hour and 20 minutes or until center is almost set. Remove from oven; gently run a knife around edge of cheesecake to loosen. Cool completely on a wire rack (about 2 hours). Cover and chill 8 hours. Remove sides of pan. Top with walnut halves. Drizzle with Honey Syrup.

Honey Syrup

Combine ½ cup honey, 2 tsp. orange blossom water, and ½ tsp. orange zest in a small saucepan. Bring to a boil over medium-high heat. Remove from heat; cool completely. Makes ½ cup.

NOTE: *Find orange blossom water at upscale food markets or cook stores.*

Mississippi Mud Cheesecake

MAKES: 16 SERVINGS · **HANDS-ON:** 20 MIN. · **TOTAL:** 9 HOURS

1. Preheat oven to 300°. Wrap outside bottom and side of 9-inch springform pan with heavy-duty foil to prevent leaking. Lightly spray inside bottom and sides of pan with cooking spray. Combine cookie crumbs and next 3 ingredients in a bowl with a pastry blender until crumbly. Press mixture into bottom of pan. Bake 12 minutes or until set. Cool crust on a wire rack 10 minutes.

2. Meanwhile, beat cream cheese, 1¼ cups sugar, flour, and vanilla at medium speed with an electric mixer until light and fluffy. Beat in eggs, 1 at a time, just until blended. Beat in melted chocolate. Pour over crust.

3. Bake at 300° for 1 hour and 15 minutes or until almost set. Turn oven off. Let cheesecake stand in oven, with oven door open at least 4 inches, for 30 minutes. Remove from oven, and gently run a knife around outer edge of cheesecake to loosen from sides of pan. (Do not remove sides of pan.) Sprinkle with marshmallows. Cool on a wire rack 30 minutes. Sprinkle with pecans.

4. Microwave frosting in a small, microwave-safe bowl at HIGH 15 seconds or until pourable. Drizzle frosting over marshmallows and pecans. Refrigerate at least 6 hours or overnight.

5. To serve, run small metal spatula around edge of pan; carefully remove foil and sides of pan.

Technique Tip

The trick to a perfect cheesecake is all about gentle and slow cooling. If you have a cool or drafty kitchen, place a large plate on top of the cheesecake while it cools on the rack.

INGREDIENTS

Vegetable cooking spray

24 thin chocolate wafer cookies (from 9-oz. package), crushed (about 1⅔ cups)

⅓ cup finely chopped pecans

2 Tbsp. sugar

6 Tbsp. butter, melted

4 (8-oz.) packages cream cheese, softened

1¼ cups sugar

2 Tbsp. all-purpose flour

1 tsp. vanilla extract

4 large eggs

2 (4-oz.) semisweet chocolate baking bars, melted and cooled

2 cups miniature marshmallows

½ cup chopped pecans, toasted

½ cup ready-to-spread chocolate frosting (from 16-oz. container)

INGREDIENTS

½ cup finely chopped
toasted pecans

Shortening

1 (4-oz.) unsweetened
chocolate baking bar

1 cup butter, softened

3¾ cups sugar, divided

11 large eggs, divided

1 cup all-purpose flour

1 cup semisweet
chocolate morsels

3 tsp. vanilla extract, divided

4 (8-oz.) packages cream
cheese, softened

Chocolate Glaze

Garnish: chocolate-dipped
pecan halves

Chocolate Fudge Cheesecakes

MAKES: 20 SERVINGS · **HANDS-ON:** 30 MIN. · **TOTAL:** 10 HOURS, 36 MIN.

A chewy brownie crust forms the base for these luscious cheesecakes.

1. Preheat oven to 325°. Sprinkle toasted pecans over bottoms of 2 greased (with shortening) and floured 9-inch springform pans.

2. Microwave chocolate baking bar in a microwave-safe bowl at MEDIUM (50% power) 1½ minutes or until melted and smooth, stirring at 30-second intervals.

3. Beat butter and 2 cups sugar at medium speed with an electric mixer until light and fluffy. Add 4 eggs, 1 at a time, beating just until blended after each addition. Add melted chocolate, beating just until blended. Add flour, beating at low speed just until blended. Stir in chocolate morsels and 1 tsp. vanilla. Divide batter between pans, spreading to edges of pan over chopped pecans.

4. Beat cream cheese at medium speed until smooth; add remaining 1¾ cups sugar, beating until blended. Add remaining 7 eggs, 1 at a time, beating just until blended after each addition. Stir in remaining 2 tsp. vanilla. Divide cream cheese mixture between each pan, spreading over chocolate batter.

5. Bake at 325° for 1 hour or until set. Remove from oven, and gently run a knife around outer edge of cheesecake to loosen from sides of pan. (Do not remove sides of pan.) Cool on wire racks 1 hour or until completely cool.

6. Spread tops of cooled cheesecakes with Chocolate Glaze; cover and chill 8 hours. Remove sides of pans.

Chocolate Glaze

Melt 1 (12-oz.) package semisweet chocolate morsels and ½ cup whipping cream in a 2-qt. microwave-safe bowl at MEDIUM (50% power) 2½ to 3 minutes or until chocolate begins to melt, stirring at 1-minute intervals. Whisk until chocolate is melted and mixture is smooth. Makes 2 cups.

Cinderella Cheesecake

MAKES: 10 TO 12 SERVINGS • **HANDS-ON:** 45 MIN. • **TOTAL:** 11 HOURS, 5 MIN.

1. Preheat oven to 350°. Microwave chocolate squares and butter in a small microwave-safe bowl at MEDIUM (50% power) 1½ minutes or until melted, stirring at 30-second intervals. Stir together flour, salt, and baking powder in a bowl.

2. Beat 2 eggs and 1 cup brown sugar at medium-high speed with an electric mixer 3 to 4 minutes or until batter forms thin ribbons when beaters are lifted. Add vanilla, bittersweet chocolate, and melted chocolate mixture, and beat just until blended. Stir in flour mixture just until combined.

3. Spread 1 cup brownie mixture on bottom of a greased (with shortening) and floured 9-inch springform pan. Bake at 350° on center oven rack 13 to 15 minutes or until set. Cool on a wire rack 10 minutes; freeze 15 minutes. Remove from freezer; spread remaining brownie batter up sides of pan to ¼ inch from top, sealing batter to bottom crust.

4. Beat cream cheese and 1 cup brown sugar at medium speed with a heavy-duty electric stand mixer until blended. Add 3 eggs, 1 at a time, beating just until yellow disappears after each addition. Beat in sour cream just until blended. Beat in peanut butter until blended. Pour filling into prepared crust. (Mixture will not completely fill crust.) Bake at 350° for 35 minutes or until center is almost set.

5. Remove from oven. Spread Sour Cream Topping over center of cheesecake, leaving a 2-inch border around edge. Bake at 350° for 1 more minute. Remove from oven, and gently run a knife around outer edge of cheesecake to loosen from sides of pan. (Do not remove sides of pan.) Cool completely on a wire rack.

6. Cover and chill 8 to 12 hours. Remove sides of pan. Top with chocolate curls and pipe peanut butter around edge.

Sour Cream Topping

Stir together ¾ cup sour cream and 2 tsp. sugar in a small bowl until smooth. Makes ¾ cup.

INGREDIENTS

3 (1-oz.) unsweetened chocolate baking squares

¼ cup unsalted butter

½ cup sifted all-purpose flour

⅛ tsp. table salt

⅛ tsp. baking powder

2 large eggs

1 cup firmly packed light brown sugar

1½ tsp. vanilla extract

½ (1-oz.) bittersweet chocolate baking square, finely chopped

Shortening

1½ (8-oz.) packages cream cheese, softened

1 cup firmly packed light brown sugar

3 large eggs

½ cup sour cream

1⅓ cups creamy peanut butter

Sour Cream Topping

Chocolate curls

Peanut butter

INGREDIENTS

1 cup chocolate wafer crumbs

2 Tbsp. sugar

3 Tbsp. butter, melted

3 (8-oz.) packages
cream cheese, softened

¾ cup sugar

¼ cup unsweetened cocoa

2 tsp. vanilla extract

3 large eggs

⅓ cup evaporated milk

⅓ cup sugar

¼ cup butter

1 large egg, lightly beaten

½ tsp. vanilla extract

½ cup coarsely chopped
toasted pecans

½ cup organic coconut chips
or flaked coconut

German Chocolate Cheesecake

MAKES: 12 SERVINGS · **HANDS-ON:** 30 MIN. · **TOTAL:** 9 HOURS, 22 MIN.

With a nod to the classic three-layer cake, this luscious cheesecake takeoff comes pretty close to perfection.

1. Preheat oven to 325°. Stir together first 3 ingredients; press into bottom of an ungreased 9-inch springform pan.

2. Bake at 325° for 10 minutes. Cool crust.

3. Increase oven temperature to 350°. Beat cream cheese and next 3 ingredients at medium speed with an electric mixer until blended. Add eggs, 1 at a time, beating just until blended after each addition. Pour into prepared crust.

4. Bake at 350° for 35 minutes. Remove cheesecake from oven, and gently run a knife around outer edge of cheesecake to loosen from sides of pan. (Do not remove sides of pan.) Cool completely in pan on a wire rack. Cover and chill 8 hours.

5. Stir together evaporated milk and next 4 ingredients in a saucepan. Cook over medium heat, stirring constantly, 7 minutes. Stir in pecans and coconut. Remove sides of pan; spread topping over cheesecake.

Serving Secret

To make this cheesecake look extra special, top with additional flaked coconut, toasted pecans, and a sprinkling of chocolate shavings.

Toffee S'mores Cheesecake

MAKES: 16 SERVINGS · **HANDS-ON:** 30 MIN. · **TOTAL:** 9 HOURS

1. Preheat oven to 325°. Wrap outside bottom and sides of 9-inch springform pan with foil to prevent leaking. Lightly spray inside bottom and side of pan with cooking spray. Combine crumbs and melted butter in a medium bowl. Press in bottom and halfway up sides of pan. Bake at 325° for 10 minutes or until set. Cool crust 10 minutes.

2. Beat cream cheese, sugar, and vanilla at medium speed with an electric mixer until smooth. Beat in eggs, 1 at a time, just until blended after each addition. Divide batter evenly between 2 bowls. Beat melted chocolate into 1 bowl; stir in ¾ cup of the sour cream. Beat remaining ¼ cup sour cream into second bowl; stir in chopped toffee candy bars. Pour toffee batter over crust. Carefully spread with chocolate batter.

3. Bake at 325° for 1 hour and 15 minutes or until almost set. Turn oven off. Let cheesecake stand in oven, with oven door open at least 4 inches, for 30 minutes. Remove from oven, and gently run a knife around outer edge of cheesecake to loosen from sides of pan. (Do not remove sides of pan.) Cool on a wire rack 30 minutes. Refrigerate at least 6 hours or overnight.

4. Just before serving, run small metal spatula around edge of pan; carefully remove foil and sides of pan. Set oven control to broil. Place cheesecake on a baking sheet. Cut marshmallows in half horizontally with dampened kitchen scissors. Place marshmallows, cut side down, on top of cheesecake. Broil about 6 inches from heat 1 to 2 minutes or until golden brown.

Technique Tip

Be sure to chill cheesecake for the full 6 hours before topping with marshmallows and serving. The marshmallows don't keep as well, so add them just before serving.

INGREDIENTS

Vegetable cooking spray

2 cups graham cracker crumbs

6 Tbsp. butter, melted

3 (8-oz.) packages cream cheese, softened

1 cup sugar

1 tsp. vanilla extract

3 large eggs

6 oz. semisweet baking chocolate, melted and cooled

1 cup sour cream

5 (1.4-oz.) chocolate-covered toffee candy bars, coarsely chopped

7 large marshmallows

Vegetable cooking spray

2 cups crushed chocolate
graham crackers
(about 18 crackers)*

⅓ cup light butter, melted

4 (8-oz.) packages ⅓-less-fat
cream cheese, softened

1 cup sugar

¼ cup coffee liqueur

1 tsp. vanilla extract

1 tsp. instant coffee granules

4 large eggs

4 (1-oz.) bittersweet
chocolate baking squares

Mocha Sauce

Lightened Chocolate-Coffee Cheesecake
with Mocha Sauce

MAKES: 10 SERVINGS · **HANDS-ON:** 20 MIN. · **TOTAL:** 7 HOURS

1. Preheat oven to 350°. Lightly grease a 9-inch springform pan with cooking spray. Stir together crushed graham crackers and melted butter; press mixture onto bottom and up sides of springform pan. Bake at 350° for 10 minutes. Cool on a wire rack. Reduce oven temperature to 325°.

2. Meanwhile, beat cream cheese and sugar at medium speed with an electric mixer until blended. Add liqueur, vanilla, and coffee granules, beating at low speed until well blended. Add eggs, 1 at a time, beating just until yellow disappears after each addition. Reserve 1 cup cream cheese batter. Pour remaining batter into prepared crust.

3. Microwave chocolate in a medium-size, microwave-safe bowl at HIGH 1 minute or until melted, stirring after 30 seconds. Stir reserved 1 cup cream cheese mixture into melted chocolate, blending well. (Mixture will be thick.) Dollop chocolate mixture on top of batter in pan; gently swirl with a knife.

4. Bake at 325° for 1 hour or until almost set. Turn oven off. Let cheesecake stand in oven, with door closed, 30 minutes. Remove from oven, and gently run a knife around outer edge of cheesecake to loosen from sides of pan. (Do not remove sides of pan.) Cool on a wire rack 1 hour. Cover and chill at least 4 hours or up to 24 hours. Remove sides of pan. Serve cheesecake with Mocha Sauce.

2 cups crushed chocolate-flavored bear-shaped graham crackers may be substituted. We tested with Nabisco Chocolate Teddy Grahams Graham Snacks.

NOTE: *We tested with Kahlúa coffee liqueur.*

Mocha Sauce

Cook 1 cup semisweet chocolate morsels, ¼ cup half-and-half, and 2 tsp. light butter in a small heavy saucepan over low heat, stirring often, 2 to 3 minutes or until smooth. Remove from heat, and stir in 3 Tbsp. strong-brewed coffee. Serve warm. Makes ¾ cup.

White Chocolate-Raspberry Cheesecake

MAKES: 12 SERVINGS · **HANDS-ON:** 22 MIN. · **TOTAL:** 9 HOURS, 20 MIN.

Raspberry preserves make a luscious surprise layer within this cheesecake.

1. Preheat oven to 350°. Combine first 3 ingredients; press crumb mixture into bottom of a lightly greased (with shortening) 9-inch springform pan. Bake 8 minutes; cool slightly.

2. Beat cream cheese at medium speed with an electric mixer until creamy; gradually add 1 cup sugar, beating well. Add eggs, 1 at a time, beating until blended after each addition. Stir in vanilla. Add melted white chocolate, beating well. Microwave raspberry preserves in a small microwave-safe bowl at HIGH 30 seconds to 1 minute or until melted; stir well.

3. Spoon half of cream cheese batter into prepared crust; spread a little more than half of melted preserves over batter, leaving a ¾-inch border. Spoon remaining cream cheese batter around edges of pan, spreading toward center. Cover remaining raspberry preserves, and chill.

4. Bake at 350° for 50 minutes or until cheesecake is just set and slightly browned. Remove from oven, and gently run a knife around outer edge of cheesecake to loosen from sides of pan. (Do not remove sides of pan.) Cool completely on a wire rack. Cover and chill at least 8 hours.

5. Reheat remaining preserves briefly in microwave to melt. Pour preserves over top of cheesecake, leaving a 1-inch border. Remove sides of pan.

Technique Tip

To remove seeds from raspberry preserves, press preserves through a fine wire-mesh strainer using the back of a spoon, if desired.

INGREDIENTS

2 cups graham cracker crumbs

3 Tbsp. sugar

½ cup butter, melted

Shortening

5 (8-oz.) packages cream cheese, softened

1 cup sugar

2 large eggs

1 Tbsp. vanilla extract

1 (12-oz.) package white chocolate morsels, melted and slightly cooled

¾ cup raspberry preserves

Garnish: fresh raspberries

2 cups cinnamon
graham cracker crumbs
(about 15 whole crackers)

½ cup melted butter

½ cup finely chopped pecans

3 (8-oz.) packages cream
cheese, softened

1⅓ cups firmly packed
light brown sugar

2 tsp. vanilla extract

3 large eggs

Caramel Apples

¼ cup apple jelly

Sweetened whipped cream

Caramel-Apple Cheesecake

MAKES: 12 SERVINGS · **HANDS-ON:** 30 MIN. · **TOTAL:** 12 HOURS, 5 MIN.

1. Preheat oven to 350°. Stir together cinnamon graham cracker crumbs and next 2 ingredients in a medium bowl until well blended. Press mixture on bottom and 1½ inches up sides of a 9-inch springform pan. Bake 10 to 12 minutes or until lightly browned. Remove to a wire rack, and cool completely (about 30 minutes).

2. Beat cream cheese, brown sugar, and vanilla at medium speed with a heavy-duty electric stand mixer until blended and smooth. Add eggs, 1 at a time, beating just until blended after each addition. Pour batter into prepared crust. Arrange Caramel Apples over cream cheese mixture.

3. Bake at 350° for 55 minutes to 1 hour and 5 minutes or until set. Remove from oven, and gently run a knife around outer edge of cheesecake to loosen from sides of pan. (Do not remove sides of pan.) Cool completely on a wire rack (about 2 hours). Cover and chill 8 to 24 hours.

4. Cook apple jelly and 1 tsp. water in a small saucepan over medium heat, stirring constantly, 2 to 3 minutes or until jelly is melted; brush over apples on top of cheesecake. Serve with whipped cream.

Caramel Apples

Peel 2¾ pounds large Granny Smith apples (about 6), and cut each one into ½-inch-thick wedges. Toss together apples and ⅓ cup brown sugar. Melt 1 Tbsp. butter in a large skillet over medium-high heat; add apple mixture, and sauté 5 to 6 minutes or until crisp-tender and golden. Cool completely (about 30 minutes).

Lemon Bar Cheesecake

MAKES: 10 TO 12 SERVINGS · **HANDS-ON:** 40 MIN. · **TOTAL:** 22 HOURS, 45 MIN.

1. Pulse first 3 ingredients in a food processor 3 or 4 times or just until blended. Add butter, and pulse 5 or 6 times or until crumbly. Whisk together egg yolks and 1 Tbsp. ice-cold water in a small bowl; add to butter mixture, and process until dough forms a ball and pulls away from sides of bowl, adding up to 1 Tbsp. remaining ice-cold water, 1 tsp. at a time, if necessary. Shape dough into a disk; wrap in plastic wrap. Chill 4 to 24 hours.

2. Roll dough into a 14-inch circle on a lightly floured surface. Fit dough into a lightly greased (with shortening) 9-inch dark springform pan, gently pressing on bottom and up sides of pan; trim and discard excess dough. Chill 30 minutes.

3. Meanwhile, preheat oven to 325°. Beat cream cheese at medium speed with an electric mixer 3 minutes or until smooth. Gradually add granulated sugar, beating until blended. Add eggs, 1 at a time, beating just until yellow disappears after each addition. Beat in vanilla. Pour two-thirds of cheesecake batter (about 4 cups) into prepared crust; dollop 1 cup lemon curd over batter in pan, and gently swirl with a knife. Spoon remaining batter into pan.

4. Bake at 325° for 1 hour to 1 hour and 10 minutes or just until center is set. Turn oven off. Let cheesecake stand in oven, with door closed, 15 minutes. Remove from oven, and gently run a knife around outer edge of cheesecake to loosen from sides of pan. (Do not remove sides of pan.) Cool completely in pan on a wire rack (about 1 hour). Cover and chill 8 to 24 hours.

5. Remove sides of pan, and transfer cheesecake to a serving platter. Spoon remaining 1 cup lemon curd over cheesecake, and, if desired, top with Candied Lemon Slices.

Candied Lemon Slices

Cut 2 small lemons into ⅛-inch-thick rounds; discard seeds. Stir together 1 cup sugar, 2 Tbsp. fresh lemon juice, and ¾ cup water in a large skillet over medium heat until sugar is dissolved. Add lemon slices, and simmer gently, keeping slices in a single layer and turning occasionally, 14 to 16 minutes or until slightly translucent and rinds are softened. Remove from heat. Place slices in a single layer in a wax paper-lined jelly-roll pan, using tongs. Cool completely (about 1 hour). Cover and chill 2 hours to 2 days. Reserve syrup for another use.

INGREDIENTS

2 cups all-purpose flour

½ cup powdered sugar

¼ tsp. table salt

½ cup cold butter, cubed

2 large egg yolks

1 to 2 Tbsp. ice-cold water

Shortening

4 (8-oz.) packages cream cheese, softened

1 cup granulated sugar

4 large eggs

2 tsp. vanilla extract

2 cups Quick and Easy Lemon Curd (page 233), divided

Candied Lemon Slices (optional)

Vegetable cooking spray

1½ cups crushed gingersnap
cookies or other crisp cookies
(about 24 cookies)

¼ cup butter, melted

3 Tbsp. sugar

3 (8-oz.) packages
cream cheese, softened

1 cup sugar

2 Tbsp. all-purpose flour

3 large eggs

⅓ cup canned coconut milk
(not cream of coconut)

2 tsp. grated lime zest

3 Tbsp. fresh lime juice

2 cups sweetened
flaked coconut

Coconut Cheesecake Squares

MAKES: 16 SQUARES · **HANDS-ON:** 15 MIN. · **TOTAL:** 3 HOURS, 50 MIN.

1. Preheat oven to 325°. Spray bottom and sides of a 9-inch square
pan with cooking spray. Mix crushed cookies, butter, and 3 Tbsp. sugar
in a small bowl until blended. Press mixture into bottom of pan. Bake
15 minutes. Cool completely.

2. Beat cream cheese, 1 cup sugar, and flour at medium speed with an
electric mixer 2 minutes or until light and fluffy. Beat in eggs, 1 at a time,
just until blended after each addition. Add coconut milk, lime zest, and
lime juice; beat at low speed until blended. Stir in 1 cup flaked coconut.
Pour over baked, cooled crust. Top with remaining 1 cup flaked coconut.

3. Bake at 325° for 45 to 50 minutes or until set. Turn oven off. Let
cheesecake stand in oven, with oven door open at least 4 inches, for
30 minutes. Remove cheesecake from oven. Cool in pan on a wire rack
1 hour. Refrigerate at least 1 hour before serving.

Quick Bite

These tropical bars get their intense coconut flavor from both coconut
milk and lots of flaked coconut. Add a little island crunch by topping
with chopped and toasted macadamia nuts.

Pineapple Upside-Down Carrot Cake

MAKES: 8 SERVINGS · **HANDS-ON:** 30 MIN. · **TOTAL:** 1 HOUR, 15 MIN.

Upgrade your classic Pineapple Upside-Down Cake by adding this unique twist: Carrot Cake. Our users loved the easy prep, and it was a huge hit with their families.

1. Preheat oven to 350°. Melt butter in a lightly greased (with shortening) 10-inch cast-iron skillet or a 9-inch round cake pan (with sides that are at least 2 inches high) over low heat. Remove from heat. Sprinkle with brown sugar. Arrange 7 pineapple slices in a single layer over brown sugar, reserving remaining pineapple slices for another use. Place 1 cherry in center of each pineapple slice.

2. Beat granulated sugar, oil, and eggs at medium speed with an electric mixer until blended. Combine flour and next 4 ingredients; gradually add to sugar mixture, beating at low speed just until blended. Stir in carrots and pecans. Spoon batter over pineapple slices.

3. Bake at 350° for 45 to 50 minutes or until a wooden pick inserted in center comes out clean. Cool in skillet on a wire rack 10 minutes. Carefully run a knife around edge of cake to loosen. Invert cake onto a serving plate, spooning any topping in skillet over cake.

Quick Bite

If you want to use fresh pineapple in this recipe, here's what you do: First, cut off the top and bottom of the pineapple. Stand it upright, and cut away the sides, leaving no rough peel remaining. Core pineapple; turn pineapple to its side, and slice into ½-inch-thick rounds.

INGREDIENTS

¼ cup butter

Shortening

⅔ cup firmly packed brown sugar

1 (20-oz.) can pineapple slices in juice, drained

7 maraschino cherries (without stems)

1 cup granulated sugar

½ cup vegetable oil

2 large eggs

1 cup all-purpose flour

1 tsp. baking powder

1 tsp. ground cinnamon

¾ tsp. baking soda

½ tsp. table salt

1½ cups grated carrots

½ cup finely chopped pecans

INGREDIENTS

½ cup chopped pecans

½ cup butter, softened
and divided

Shortening

1 cup firmly packed light
brown sugar

2 Tbsp. rum

2 ripe bananas

¾ cup granulated sugar

2 large eggs

¾ cup milk

½ cup sour cream

1 tsp. vanilla extract

2 cups all-purpose baking mix

¼ tsp. ground cinnamon

Bananas Foster
Upside-Down Cake

MAKES: 8 SERVINGS · **HANDS-ON:** 20 MIN. · **TOTAL:** 1 HOUR, 18 MIN.

One quick flip and this Bananas Foster Upside-Down Cake tumbles from the skillet perfectly golden and party-ready.

1. Preheat oven to 350°. Bake pecans in a single layer 8 to 10 minutes or until toasted and fragrant, stirring once.

2. Melt ¼ cup butter in a lightly greased (with shortening) 10-inch cast-iron skillet or 9-inch round cake pan (with sides that are at least 2 inches high) over low heat. Remove from heat; stir in brown sugar and rum.

3. Cut bananas diagonally into ¼-inch-thick slices; arrange in concentric circles over brown sugar mixture. Sprinkle pecans over bananas.

4. Beat granulated sugar and remaining ¼ cup butter at medium speed with an electric mixer until blended. Add eggs, 1 at a time, beating just until blended after each addition. Add milk and next 2 ingredients; beat just until blended. Beat in baking mix and cinnamon until blended. (Batter will be slightly lumpy.) Pour batter over mixture in skillet. Place skillet on a foil-lined jelly-roll pan.

5. Bake at 350° for 40 to 45 minutes or until a wooden pick inserted in center comes out clean. Cool in skillet on a wire rack 10 minutes. Run a knife around edge to loosen. Invert cake onto a serving plate, spooning any topping in skillet over cake.

Peach Upside-Down Cake

MAKES: 8 TO 12 SERVINGS · **HANDS-ON:** 20 MIN. · **TOTAL:** 1 HOUR, 10 MIN.

1. Preheat oven to 350°. Line a baking sheet with parchment paper. Toss peaches with lemon juice. Sift together flour, baking powder, and baking soda.

2. Cook ½ cup granulated sugar in a 10-inch cast-iron skillet over medium heat 10 minutes or until sugar melts and turns a deep amber color. Remove from heat. Immediately add ¼ cup butter, stirring vigorously. Spread caramelized sugar to coat bottom of skillet evenly, and sprinkle with brown sugar. Arrange peach wedges in concentric circles over sugar mixture, overlapping as needed.

3. Split vanilla bean lengthwise, and scrape out seeds into bowl of a heavy-duty electric stand mixer. Beat vanilla seeds, remaining ¾ cup granulated sugar, and remaining ½ cup butter at medium speed until smooth. Add eggs, 1 at a time, beating until blended after each addition. Add sour cream, beating until blended. Gradually add sifted flour mixture, beating at low speed just until blended and stopping to scrape bowl as needed. Spoon batter over peaches in skillet. Place skillet on prepared baking sheet.

4. Bake at 350° for 40 to 45 minutes or until golden brown and a wooden pick inserted in center comes out clean. Cool in skillet on a wire rack 10 minutes. Run a knife around edge to loosen.

5. Carefully invert cake onto a serving plate, spooning any remaining liquid over cake.

Quick Bite

Be sure to use cake flour—not self-rising—for this recipe. Cake flour has less gluten than all-purpose flour and will result in a more tender crumb.

INGREDIENTS

Parchment paper

4 medium peaches (about 1½ lb.), unpeeled and cut into ⅓-inch-thick wedges

2 Tbsp. fresh lemon juice (about 1 large lemon)

1 cup cake flour

¾ tsp. baking powder

¼ tsp. baking soda

1¼ cups granulated sugar, divided

¾ cup unsalted butter, at room temperature and divided

½ cup firmly packed light brown sugar

1 vanilla bean

2 large eggs

½ cup sour cream

Garnish: sweetened whipped cream

INGREDIENTS

Vegetable cooking spray

¼ cup butter

1 cup firmly packed brown sugar

2 medium pears, peeled
and thinly sliced

1 box gingerbread cake
and cookie mix

1 cup stout beer

1 large egg

Beer-Braised Pears

Upside-Down Pear Gingerbread Cake
with Beer-Braised Pears

MAKES: 8 SERVINGS · **HANDS-ON:** 15 MIN. · **TOTAL:** 50 MIN.

1. Preheat oven to 350°. Lightly grease a 9-inch springform pan with cooking spray.

2. Microwave butter in a small, microwave-safe bowl at HIGH about 1 minute or until melted; stir in 1 cup brown sugar. Spread in bottom of pan; arrange 2 sliced pears over brown sugar mixture.

3. Stir cake mix, 1 cup beer, and egg in a large bowl until well blended. Spoon over pears. Bake at 350° for 25 to 30 minutes or until a wooden pick inserted in center comes out clean.

4. Cool in skillet on a wire rack 10 minutes. Run a knife around edge to loosen. Invert cake onto a serving plate. Serve warm cake with Beer-Braised Pears.

Beer-Braised Pears

Cook 5 peeled and sliced medium pears, 1 cup firmly packed brown sugar, and ¼ cup stout beer in a 12-inch skillet over medium-high heat about 15 minutes, stirring occasionally, until pears are tender. Remove from heat; cover to keep warm.

Quick Bite

The rule when cooking with alcohol is cook with what you would drink. This is true for wine and beer. For this cake, use a stout beer that you enjoy drinking for the best results.

Fig Upside-Down Cake

MAKES: 6 TO 8 SERVINGS · **HANDS-ON:** 28 MIN. · **TOTAL:** 1 HOUR, 8 MIN.

1. Preheat oven to 350°. Melt butter in a 10-inch cast-iron skillet over medium-low heat; sprinkle brown sugar over butter. Remove from heat. Arrange figs, cut sides down, over sugar mixture; sprinkle with walnuts.

2. Beat 3 egg yolks at high speed with an electric mixer until thick and pale; gradually add 1 cup granulated sugar, beating well. Stir together flour and next 4 ingredients; add to egg mixture alternately with milk, beginning and ending with flour mixture. Stir in vanilla.

3. Beat egg whites at high speed with an electric mixer until stiff peaks form; fold egg whites into batter. Pour batter over figs in skillet.

4. Bake at 350° for 38 to 40 minutes or until a wooden pick inserted in center comes out clean. Cool in skillet on a wire rack 10 minutes; invert cake onto a serving platter, scraping any syrup from bottom of skillet onto cake.

5. Beat whipping cream and port, if desired, until soft peaks form. Serve cake warm or at room temperature with whipped cream.

Quick Bite

Port is a blend of a still wine, typically red, and brandy. Ruby port gets its name from the distinct ruby color created from the mix of grapes used to make this variety. Although the port is an exceptional addition to the whipped cream and pairs beautifully with the cake, it can be omitted.

INGREDIENTS

½ cup butter

1 cup firmly packed brown sugar

12 fresh Brown Turkey or Mission figs, halved

½ cup chopped walnuts

2 large eggs, separated

1 large egg yolk

1 cup granulated sugar

1 cup all-purpose flour

1 tsp. baking powder

1 tsp. chopped fresh rosemary

1 tsp. lemon zest

¼ tsp. table salt

¼ cup milk

½ tsp. vanilla extract

¾ cup whipping cream

2 Tbsp. ruby port (optional)

INGREDIENTS

1 large egg

½ cup fat-free milk

½ cup plain fat-free yogurt

3 Tbsp. vegetable oil

2 cups all-purpose flour

½ cup granulated sugar

4 tsp. baking powder

½ tsp. table salt

1½ cups frozen blueberries

1 Tbsp. all-purpose flour

Shortening

2 Tbsp. turbinado sugar

2 Tbsp. sliced almonds

¼ tsp. ground cinnamon

Blueberry Coffee Cake

MAKES: 10 SERVINGS · **HANDS-ON:** 20 MIN. · **TOTAL:** 1 HOUR

There's nothing like waking up to the aroma of freshly baked breakfast treats—especially with plump blueberries! Sliced almonds and turbinado sugar add a bit of crunch over the tender coffee cake.

1. Preheat oven to 400°. Whisk together first 4 ingredients in a large bowl.

2. Sift together flour and next 3 ingredients in another bowl. Stir flour mixture into egg mixture just until dry ingredients are moistened.

3. Toss 1¼ cups blueberries in 1 Tbsp. flour; fold into batter. Pour into a lightly greased (with shortening) 9-inch springform pan. Sprinkle with remaining ¼ cup blueberries.

4. Stir together 2 Tbsp. turbinado sugar, sliced almonds, and cinnamon; sprinkle over batter.

5. Bake at 400° for 25 to 30 minutes or until a wooden pick inserted in center comes out clean. Cool in pan on a wire rack 15 minutes; remove sides of pan.

Quick Bite

Combine the dry ingredients the night before for a quick morning start. Serve this cake warm or at room temperature.

Caramel Apple Coffee Cake

MAKES: 8 TO 10 SERVINGS · **HANDS-ON:** 35 MINUTES · **TOTAL:** 4 HOURS, 50 MIN.

1. Preheat oven to 350°. Melt 2 Tbsp. butter in a large skillet over medium-high heat; add apples, and sauté 5 minutes or until softened. Remove from heat; cool completely (about 30 minutes).

2. Beat butter at medium speed with an electric mixer until creamy; gradually add sugar, beating well. Add eggs, 1 at a time, beating until blended after each addition.

3. Combine flour, baking powder, and salt; add to butter mixture alternately with milk, beginning and ending with flour mixture. Beat at low speed until blended after each addition. Stir in vanilla. Pour batter into a greased (with shortening) and floured shiny 9-inch springform pan; top with apples. Drizzle with ½ cup Caramel Sauce; sprinkle with Streusel Topping.

4. Bake at 350° for 45 minutes. Cover loosely with aluminum foil to prevent excessive browning; bake 25 to 30 minutes or until center is set. (A wooden pick will not come out clean.) Cool in pan on a wire rack 30 minutes; remove sides of pan. Cool completely on wire rack (about 1½ hours). Drizzle with remaining ½ cup Caramel Sauce.

Caramel Sauce

Bring 1 cup firmly packed light brown sugar, ½ cup butter, ¼ cup whipping cream, and ¼ cup honey to a boil in a medium saucepan over medium-high heat, stirring constantly; boil, stirring constantly, 2 minutes. Remove from heat, and cool 15 minutes before serving. Store in an airtight container in refrigerator up to 1 week. To reheat, microwave at HIGH 10 to 15 seconds or just until warm; stir until smooth. Makes about 1½ cups.

Streusel Topping

Stir together 1½ cups all-purpose flour, 1 cup chopped pecans, ½ cup melted butter, ½ cup firmly packed light brown sugar, ¼ cup granulated sugar, 1½ tsp. ground cinnamon, and ¼ tsp. table salt until blended. Let stand 30 minutes or until firm enough to crumble into small pieces.

INGREDIENTS

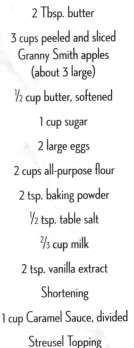

2 Tbsp. butter

3 cups peeled and sliced Granny Smith apples (about 3 large)

½ cup butter, softened

1 cup sugar

2 large eggs

2 cups all-purpose flour

2 tsp. baking powder

½ tsp. table salt

⅔ cup milk

2 tsp. vanilla extract

Shortening

1 cup Caramel Sauce, divided

Streusel Topping

INGREDIENTS

Shortening

Parchment paper

3 large lemons

2 cups all-purpose flour

1¼ cups granulated sugar

½ tsp. table salt

½ cup very cold butter, cubed

1 tsp. baking powder

½ tsp. baking soda

¾ cup buttermilk*

1 large egg

1½ tsp. chopped fresh rosemary

1 (10-oz.) jar lemon curd

Powdered sugar

Garnishes: fresh rosemary sprigs, lemon slices, lemon zest curls

Lemon-Rosemary Coffee Cake

MAKES: 8 TO 10 SERVINGS · **HANDS-ON:** 25 MIN. · **TOTAL:** 2 HOURS, 20 MIN.

Perfect for brunch or tea, moist Lemon-Rosemary Coffee Cake is a perfect pick. Fresh rosemary complements the lemony flavor in this coffee cake.

1. Preheat oven to 350°. Lightly grease (with shortening) bottom and sides of a 9-inch springform pan. Line bottom of pan with parchment paper.

2. Grate zest from lemons to equal 1 Tbsp. Cut lemons in half; squeeze juice from lemons into a bowl to equal 5 Tbsp. Reserve zest and 1 Tbsp. lemon juice.

3. Combine flour, granulated sugar, and salt in bowl of a food processor; pulse 3 to 4 times or until blended. Add butter; pulse 6 to 7 times or until mixture resembles coarse crumbs. Reserve 1 cup flour mixture.

4. Transfer remaining flour mixture to bowl of a heavy-duty electric stand mixer. Add baking powder and baking soda; beat at low speed until well blended. Add buttermilk, egg, and ¼ cup lemon juice; beat at medium speed 1½ to 2 minutes or until batter is thoroughly blended, stopping to scrape bowl as needed. Stir in rosemary. Spoon half of batter into prepared pan.

5. Whisk lemon curd in a small bowl about 1 minute or until loosened and smooth; carefully spread over batter in pan. Top with remaining half of batter. Stir together reserved lemon zest, 1 Tbsp. lemon juice, and 1 cup flour mixture; sprinkle lemon zest mixture over batter in pan.

6. Bake at 350° for 45 to 50 minutes or until a long wooden pick inserted in center comes out clean.

7. Let cool in pan on a wire rack 10 minutes. Gently run a sharp knife around edge of cake to loosen; remove sides of pan. Cool cake completely on wire rack (about 1 hour). Dust with powdered sugar just before serving.

*Greek yogurt may be substituted for buttermilk.

Banana-Pecan Coffee Cake

MAKES: 8 TO 10 SERVINGS · **HANDS-ON:** 20 MIN. · **TOTAL:** 1 HOUR, 23 MIN.

This decadent coffee cake recipe has the added convenience of a baking mix that's enhanced with cinnamon, sugar, eggs, and sour cream.

1. Melt ¼ cup butter in a 10-inch cast-iron skillet over low heat; stir in rum. Sprinkle brown sugar evenly over butter mixture. Remove from heat.

2. Sprinkle pecans evenly over brown sugar mixture. Cut bananas in half crosswise; cut each half lengthwise into 3 slices. Arrange banana slices in a spoke pattern over pecans. Cut 6 cherries in half. Place 1 cherry half between each banana slice. Place remaining whole cherry in center of skillet.

3. Preheat oven to 350°. Beat remaining ¼ cup butter and ½ cup granulated sugar in a large bowl at medium speed with an electric mixer until blended. Add egg yolks, 1 at a time, beating just until blended after each addition. Add milk, sour cream, and vanilla, beating just until blended. Combine baking mix and cinnamon. Add cinnamon mixture to milk mixture, beating just until blended.

4. Beat egg whites in a large bowl with an electric mixer until soft peaks form. Gradually beat in remaining ¼ cup granulated sugar until stiff peaks form. Fold into batter. Spread batter evenly over bananas in skillet.

5. Bake at 350° for 45 to 50 minutes or until a wooden pick inserted in center comes out clean. Cool in skillet on wire rack 10 minutes. Run a knife around edge to loosen. Invert cake onto a serving plate. Serve warm with whipped cream, if desired.

NOTE: *We tested with Bisquick All-Purpose Baking Mix.*

INGREDIENTS

½ cup butter, softened and divided

2 Tbsp. rum

1 cup firmly packed light brown sugar

½ cup chopped pecans, toasted

2 medium-size ripe bananas

7 maraschino cherries

¾ cup granulated sugar, divided

2 large eggs, separated

¾ cup milk

½ cup sour cream

1 tsp. vanilla extract

2 cups all-purpose baking mix

¼ tsp. ground cinnamon

Whipped cream (optional)

INGREDIENTS

2 cups all-purpose flour

2 cups firmly packed
light brown sugar

¾ cup butter, cubed

Shortening

1 cup sour cream

1 large egg, lightly beaten

1 tsp. baking soda

3 Tbsp. granulated sugar

1 tsp. ground cinnamon

1 cup chopped pecans

Brown Sugar-Pecan Coffee Cake

MAKES: 12 SERVINGS · **HANDS-ON:** 15 MIN. · **TOTAL:** 45 MIN.

This sweet brown sugar-rich cake is the perfect addition to any holiday brunch spread.

1. Preheat oven to 350°. Stir together flour and brown sugar in a large bowl. Cut ¾ cup butter into flour mixture with a pastry blender until crumbly. Press 2¾ cups crumb mixture evenly on the bottom of a lightly greased (with shortening) 13- x 9-inch pan.

2. Stir together sour cream, egg, and baking soda; add to remaining crumb mixture, stirring just until dry ingredients are moistened. Stir together granulated sugar and cinnamon. Pour sour cream mixture over crumb crust in pan; sprinkle evenly with cinnamon mixture and pecans.

3. Bake at 350° for 25 to 30 minutes or until a wooden pick inserted in center comes out clean.

Quick Bite

This coffee cake is super simple, thanks to an ingenious crumble crust that doubles as part of the filling, too!

Apricot-Almond Coffee Cake

MAKES: 15 SERVINGS • **HANDS-ON:** 20 MIN. • **TOTAL:** 1 HOUR, 10 MIN.

1. Preheat oven to 350°. In a medium bowl, beat cream cheese, apricot preserves, and 1 Tbsp. cake mix at medium-low speed with an electric mixer just until blended.

2. In another bowl, beat sour cream, milk, eggs, almond extract, and remaining cake mix at low speed with an electric mixer 30 seconds or until blended. Increase speed to medium, and beat 3 more minutes.

3. Pour sour cream batter into a lightly greased (with shortening) 13- x 9-inch pan. Dollop cream cheese mixture by rounded tablespoonfuls evenly over batter. Swirl batter gently with a knife. Sprinkle almonds over top.

4. Bake at 350° for 25 to 30 minutes or until golden and a wooden pick inserted in center comes out clean. Cool in pan on a wire rack 20 minutes. Drizzle Glaze over slightly warm cake or individual pieces.

NOTE: *We tested with Betty Crocker Pound Cake Mix.*

Glaze

Stir together 1 cup powdered sugar, ½ tsp. vanilla extract, and 1 Tbsp. milk in a small bowl until smooth. Stir in up to 1 Tbsp. additional milk, if necessary, for desired consistency. Makes ⅓ cup.

Technique Tip

If using a hand mixer, follow directions above. If using a stand mixer, prepare sour cream batter first, transfer to prepared pan, and then make the cream cheese mixture.

INGREDIENTS

4 oz. cream cheese, softened

½ cup apricot preserves

1 (16-oz.) package pound cake mix, divided

1 (8-oz.) container sour cream

½ cup milk

2 large eggs

½ tsp. almond extract

Shortening

½ cup sliced almonds

Glaze

INGREDIENTS

1 (16-oz.) container sour cream

⅓ cup sugar

¼ cup butter

1 tsp. table salt

2 (¼-oz.) envelopes active dry yeast

½ cup warm water (100° to 110°)

1 Tbsp. sugar

2 large eggs, lightly beaten

6 to 6½ cups bread flour

Shortening

⅓ cup butter, softened

½ cup sugar

1½ tsp. ground cinnamon

Creamy Glaze

Purple, green, and gold sparkling sugars

King Cake

MAKES: 2 CAKES (ABOUT 18 SERVINGS EACH) • **HANDS-ON:** 30 MIN. • **TOTAL:** 2 HOURS, 30 MIN.

If you like, hide a heat- and food-safe plastic baby (or a raisin or nut) in the dough of this Mardi Gras treat for one lucky (or unlucky) diner to find.

1. Cook first 4 ingredients in a medium saucepan over low heat, stirring often, until butter melts. Set aside; cool to 100° to 110°. Stir together yeast, ½ cup warm water, and 1 Tbsp. sugar in a 1-cup glass measuring cup; let stand 5 minutes.

2. Beat sour cream mixture, yeast mixture, eggs, and 2 cups flour at medium speed with a heavy-duty electric stand mixer until smooth. Reduce speed to low, and gradually add enough remaining flour (4 to 4½ cups) until a soft dough forms. Turn dough out onto a lightly floured surface; knead until smooth and elastic (about 10 minutes). Place in a well-greased (with shortening) bowl, turning to grease top. Cover and let rise in a warm place (85°), free from drafts, 1 hour or until dough is doubled in bulk.

3. Punch down dough, and divide in half. Roll each portion into a 22- x 12-inch rectangle. Spread ⅓ cup softened butter evenly on each rectangle, leaving a 1-inch border. Stir together ½ cup sugar and cinnamon, and sprinkle evenly over butter on each rectangle.

4. Roll up each dough rectangle, jelly-roll fashion, starting at 1 long side. Place 1 dough roll, seam side down, on a lightly greased (with shortening) baking sheet. Bring ends of roll together to form an oval ring, moistening and pinching edges together to seal. Repeat with second dough roll. Cover and let rise in a warm place (85°), free from drafts, 20 to 30 minutes or until doubled in bulk.

5. Preheat oven to 375°. Bake 14 to 16 minutes or until golden. Slightly cool cakes on pans on wire racks (about 10 minutes). Drizzle Creamy Glaze evenly over warm cakes; sprinkle with colored sugars, alternating colors and forming bands. Cool completely.

Creamy Glaze

Stir together 3 cups powdered sugar, 3 Tbsp. melted butter, 2 Tbsp. fresh lemon juice, and ¼ tsp. vanilla extract. Stir in 2 Tbsp. milk, adding additional milk, 1 tsp. at a time, until spreading consistency. Makes 1½ cups.

PRETTY POUND
CAKES

Pound Cake from Heaven

MAKES: 12 SERVINGS · **HANDS-ON:** 15 MIN. · **TOTAL:** 3 HOURS, 30 MIN.

In the South, we love a good pound cake. This one is positively heavenly—sweet and rich but still, somehow, light as a cloud.

1. Preheat oven to 350°. Place butter in the bowl of a heavy-duty electric stand mixer, and beat at medium speed until light and fluffy (about 6 minutes). Gradually add sugar, beating until blended. Beat 1 more minute. Add eggs, 1 at a time, beating just until yellow disappears after each addition.

2. Combine flour and next 2 ingredients. Combine evaporated milk and cream; add to butter mixture alternately with flour mixture, beginning and ending with flour mixture. Beat at low speed just until blended after each addition, stopping to scrape down sides as needed. Stir in vanilla. Pour batter into a greased (with shortening) and floured 10-inch (16-cup) tube pan.

3. Bake at 350° for 1 hour and 15 minutes or until a long wooden pick inserted in center comes out clean. Cool in pan on a wire rack 1 hour; remove from pan to wire rack, and cool completely (about 1 hour).

Technique Tip

Creaming the butter and sugar is the most important step when making a pound cake. Give it time to whip up light and fluffy, and scrape down the sides often when adding eggs.

INGREDIENTS

1½ cups unsalted butter, softened

3 cups sugar

5 large eggs

3 cups all-purpose soft-wheat flour

1 tsp. baking powder

¼ tsp. table salt

1 (5-oz.) can evaporated milk

⅔ cup heavy cream

1 Tbsp. vanilla extract

Shortening

Garnishes: sweetened whipped cream, fresh strawberries

1⅓ cups butter, softened

2½ cups sugar

6 large eggs

3 cups all-purpose flour

½ cup buttermilk

1 tsp. vanilla extract

Shortening

Buttermilk Custard Sauce

Garnishes: blueberries, raspberries, mint sprigs

Buttermilk Pound Cake
with Buttermilk Custard Sauce

MAKES: 12 SERVINGS · **HANDS-ON:** 15 MIN. · **TOTAL:** 2 HOURS, 45 MIN., INCLUDING SAUCE

1. Preheat oven to 325°. Beat butter at medium speed with a heavy-duty electric stand mixer until creamy. Gradually add sugar, beating at medium speed until light and fluffy. Add eggs, 1 at a time, beating just until blended after each addition.

2. Add flour to butter mixture alternately with buttermilk, beginning and ending with flour. Beat at low speed just until blended after each addition. Stir in vanilla. Pour batter into a greased (with shortening) and floured 10-inch (16-cup) tube pan.

3. Bake at 325° for 1 hour and 5 minutes to 1 hour and 10 minutes or until a long wooden pick inserted in center comes out clean. Cool in pan on a wire rack 10 to 15 minutes; remove from pan to wire rack, and cool completely (about 1 hour). Serve with Buttermilk Custard Sauce.

Buttermilk Custard Sauce

Whisk together 2 cups buttermilk, ½ cup sugar, 1 Tbsp. cornstarch, and 3 large egg yolks in a heavy 3-qt. saucepan. Bring to a boil over medium heat, whisking constantly, and boil 1 minute. Remove from heat, and stir in 1 tsp. vanilla extract. Serve warm or cold. Store leftovers in an airtight container in refrigerator for up to 1 week. Makes about 2⅓ cups.

Quick Bite

Buttermilk is an important ingredient for this cake and the sauce. However, if you don't have any, don't fret! Just stir 1 Tbsp. lemon juice into 1 cup of milk, and let stand 5 minutes.

Caramel-Frosted Pound Cake

MAKES: 16 SERVINGS · **HANDS-ON:** 45 MIN. · **TOTAL:** 4 HOURS

This cake combines the two quintessential Southern cakes—pound cake and caramel cake—into one. The result is a surefire crowd-pleaser.

1. Preheat oven to 325°. Grease and flour a 10-inch (16-cup) tube pan with shortening.

2. Beat 3 cups sugar and 1 cup butter at medium speed with an electric mixer 5 minutes or until light and fluffy. Add eggs, 1 at a time, beating well after each addition. Beat in vanilla and almond extract. Add flour alternately with whipping cream, beginning and ending with flour, beating well after each addition. Beat at medium speed 2 minutes. Pour batter into pan.

3. Bake at 325° for 1 hour and 15 minutes or until a long wooden pick inserted in center comes out clean. Cool in pan on a wire rack 10 to 15 minutes; remove from pan to wire rack, and cool completely (about 1 hour).

4. Using an offset spatula and working quickly, spread Caramel Frosting over cake (frosting will harden as it cools). Let stand 30 minutes before slicing.

Caramel Frosting

Heat ¼ cup sugar in an 8- or 10-inch skillet over medium heat until amber colored, about 6 minutes, shaking pan occasionally (do not stir). Meanwhile, heat 1¼ cups sugar, ½ cup butter, and ½ cup milk in a 3-qt. saucepan to boiling over medium-high heat. Gradually stir in caramelized sugar with a whisk; cook until a candy thermometer registers 232°F. Remove from heat; cool, about 20 minutes, stirring occasionally, until frosting is smooth and spreadable.

INGREDIENTS

Shortening

3 cups sugar

1 cup butter, softened

6 large eggs

2 tsp. vanilla extract

1 tsp. almond extract

3 cups all-purpose flour

1 cup whipping cream

Caramel Frosting

6 large eggs, separated

1¼ cups granulated sugar

1 tsp. coffee extract

2 cups all-purpose flour

1 Tbsp. baking powder

1 Tbsp. finely ground coffee

1 tsp. kosher salt

¾ cup butter, melted

½ cup milk

3 cups firmly packed light
brown sugar

3 cups brewed coffee

½ cup rum*

Garnishes: whipped cream,
fresh raspberries,
powdered sugar

Coffee Baba au Rhum

MAKES: 12 SERVINGS · **HANDS-ON:** 35 MIN. · **TOTAL:** 2 HOURS, 10 MIN.

This sophisticated French confection became très chic in America when Julia Child was the crème de la crème of cooks. This recipe is based on the original yeast recipe, but we've made a quicker and easier version that'll earn "ooh la las" from your luncheon or teatime crowd. Whipped egg whites give it baba au rhum's signature airy crumb, the perfect texture to soak up a divine rum syrup.

1. Preheat oven to 350°. Whisk together yolks and granulated sugar until mixture is thick and pale (about 2 minutes). Stir in coffee extract. Sift together flour and next 3 ingredients; gently stir into yolk mixture until just blended. Stir in butter and milk until just blended.

2. Whisk egg whites until stiff peaks form. Fold one-third of egg whites into yolk mixture. Fold in remaining egg whites. Pour into a well-buttered 10-inch (12-cup) Bundt pan.

3. Bake at 350° for 50 minutes or until a long wooden pick inserted in center comes out clean. Cool in pan on a wire rack 10 minutes. (Do not remove from pan.)

4. Meanwhile, bring brown sugar and brewed coffee to a boil in a medium saucepan. Reduce heat to low, and simmer, stirring occasionally, 20 minutes. Remove from heat; stir in rum. Reserve 2 cups syrup. Return pan to stove-top; cook over medium-low heat, stirring occasionally, 15 minutes or until slightly thickened.

5. Pierce cake 10 to 15 times using a skewer. Pour reserved 2 cups thin syrup over cake. Let stand 15 minutes. Invert cake onto a serving platter. Spoon desired amount of thickened syrup over cake. Reserve remaining syrup for another use (such as topping pancakes).

*The rum is optional. Replace it with an additional ½ cup brewed coffee, if desired.

Hummingbird Bundt Cake

MAKES: 10 TO 12 SERVINGS · **HANDS-ON:** 20 MIN. · **TOTAL:** 3 HOURS, 45 MIN., INCLUDING GLAZE

From pineapple to cream cheese, Hummingbird Bundt Cake has all the same ingredients as the popular layer cake but is simplified as an easy-to-take Bundt cake!

1. Preheat oven to 350°. Stir together flour and next 4 ingredients in a large bowl; stir in eggs and next 4 ingredients, stirring just until dry ingredients are moistened. Sprinkle 1 cup toasted pecans into a greased (with shortening) and floured 10-inch (12-cup) Bundt pan. Spoon batter over pecans.

2. Bake at 350° for 1 hour to 1 hour and 10 minutes or until a long wooden pick inserted in center comes out clean. Cool cake in pan on a wire rack 15 minutes; remove from pan to wire rack, and cool completely (about 2 hours).

3. When cake has cooled, make glaze. Immediately pour glaze over cooled cake, and sprinkle with remaining ½ cup toasted pecans.

Cream Cheese Glaze

Process 4 oz. cream cheese, 2 cups sifted powdered sugar, 1 tsp. vanilla extract, and 1 Tbsp. milk in a food processor until well blended. Add 1 Tbsp. milk, 1 tsp. at a time, processing until smooth. Makes about 2 cups.

Technique Tip

Don't begin making the Cream Cheese Glaze until the cake has cooled completely. You need to pour icing over the cake immediately, which you cannot do if the cake is warm.

INGREDIENTS

3 cups all-purpose flour

2 cups sugar

1 tsp. baking soda

1 tsp. ground cinnamon

½ tsp. table salt

3 large eggs, lightly beaten

1¾ cups mashed ripe bananas (about 4 large)

1 (8-oz.) can crushed pineapple, undrained

¾ cup canola oil

1½ tsp. vanilla extract

1½ cups chopped toasted pecans

Shortening

Cream Cheese Glaze

INGREDIENTS

1½ cups sugar

1 cup butter, softened

4 large eggs

3 cups all-purpose flour

2 Tbsp. unsweetened cocoa

1 tsp. ground cinnamon

½ tsp. table salt

½ tsp. ground allspice

¼ tsp. ground nutmeg

1 cup buttermilk

1 tsp. baking soda

1½ cups seedless
blackberry jam

2 tsp. vanilla extract

1½ cups chopped
toasted pecans

Shortening

Caramel Glaze

Garnishes: fresh mint sprigs,
blackberries

Tennessee Jam Bundt

MAKES: 12 SERVINGS · **HANDS-ON:** 30 MIN. · **TOTAL:** 4 HOURS, 30 MIN.

1. Preheat oven to 325°. Beat granulated sugar and 1 cup butter at medium speed with a heavy-duty electric stand mixer until light and fluffy. Add eggs, 1 at a time, beating just until blended after each addition.

2. Stir together flour and next 5 ingredients. Stir together buttermilk and baking soda. Add flour mixture to butter mixture alternately with buttermilk mixture, beginning and ending with flour mixture. Beat at low speed just until blended after each addition. Add jam and vanilla, and beat just until blended. Stir in pecans. Grease (with shortening) and flour a 12-cup Bundt pan. Pour batter into prepared pan.

3. Bake at 325° for 1 hour to 1 hour and 15 minutes or until a long wooden pick inserted in center comes out clean. Cool cake in pan on a wire rack 20 minutes; remove from pan to wire rack, and cool completely (about 2 hours). Immediately pour Caramel Glaze over cooled cake.

Caramel Glaze

Bring ½ cup firmly packed dark brown sugar, ½ cup whipping cream, and ¼ cup butter to a boil in a 2-qt. saucepan over medium heat, whisking constantly; boil, whisking constantly, 1 minute. Remove from heat; stir in 1 tsp. vanilla extract. Gradually whisk in 1¼ cups powdered sugar until smooth. Gently stir 3 to 5 minutes or until mixture begins to cool and thicken. Makes about 1½ cups.

Serving Secret

Although this Bundt is packed with flavor, it has a humble appearance. Serve it on a gilded plate or pedestal, and surround it with plump blackberries and fresh mint sprigs for a party-worthy look.

Black Forest Pound Cake

MAKES: 10 SERVINGS · **HANDS-ON:** 30 MIN. · **TOTAL:** 3 HOURS, 15 MIN.

1. Preheat oven to 325°. Beat butter at medium speed with a heavy-duty electric stand mixer until creamy. Gradually add 1⅓ cups granulated sugar and ⅔ cup brown sugar, beating until light and fluffy (about 5 minutes). Add eggs, 1 at a time, beating just until blended after each addition. Beat in 1 tsp. vanilla.

2. Whisk together flour and next 3 ingredients. Add to butter mixture alternately with sour cream, beginning and ending with flour mixture. Beat at low speed just until blended after each addition. Stir in chopped chocolate.

3. Pour batter into a greased (with shortening) and floured 10-inch round cake pan (with sides that are 3 inches high).

4. Bake at 325° for 1 hour and 10 minutes to 1 hour and 20 minutes or until a long wooden pick inserted in center comes out clean. Cool in pan on a wire rack 15 minutes. Remove from pan to wire rack; cool completely (about 1 hour).

5. Place cake on a serving plate or cake stand. Slowly pour Cherry Sauce over cake. Beat heavy cream, 1 Tbsp. granulated sugar, and remaining ½ tsp. vanilla at medium-high speed until soft peaks form. Dollop whipped cream onto cake, and sprinkle with shaved chocolate.

Cherry Sauce

Stir together 2 (12-oz.) packages frozen cherries, ⅓ cup sugar, ⅓ cup cold water, and 2 tsp. cornstarch in a medium saucepan. Cook over medium-low heat, stirring often, 12 to 15 minutes or until thickened. Remove from heat, and stir in 2 Tbsp. Kirsch or brandy, ½ tsp. vanilla extract, and a pinch of table salt. Cool completely (about 1 hour). Makes 1⅓ cups.

INGREDIENTS

⅔ cup butter, softened

1⅓ cups granulated sugar

⅔ cup firmly packed
dark brown sugar

4 large eggs

1½ tsp. vanilla extract, divided

1½ cups cake flour

½ cup unsweetened cocoa

½ tsp. table salt

¼ tsp. baking soda

¾ cup sour cream

3 (1-oz.) bittersweet
chocolate baking squares,
finely chopped

Shortening

Cherry Sauce

1¼ cups heavy cream

1 Tbsp. granulated sugar

Shaved bittersweet chocolate

INGREDIENTS

⅔ cup chopped pecans

¼ cup butter, softened

2 Tbsp. granulated sugar

Shortening

2¾ cups all-purpose flour

1 tsp. baking soda

1 tsp. table salt

1 cup butter, softened

1 cup firmly packed dark brown sugar

½ cup granulated sugar

1 Tbsp. vanilla extract

4 large eggs

1 cup buttermilk

1 (12-oz.) package semisweet chocolate mini-morsels

Powdered Sugar Glaze

Chocolate Chip Bundt Cake

MAKES: 12 SERVINGS • **HANDS-ON:** 25 MIN. • **TOTAL:** 2 HOURS, 25 MIN.

This moist, chocolaty cake is even better after standing for a day. Let it "season" to develop more flavor.

1. Preheat oven to 350°. Stir together first 3 ingredients in a small bowl, using a fork. Sprinkle into a greased (with shortening) and floured 10-inch (12-cup) Bundt pan.

2. Whisk together flour, baking soda, and salt.

3. Beat butter, brown sugar, granulated sugar, and vanilla at medium speed with a heavy-duty electric stand mixer 3 to 5 minutes or until fluffy. Add eggs, 1 at a time, beating just until blended. Add flour mixture alternately with buttermilk, beginning and ending with flour mixture. Beat at low speed just until blended after each addition, stopping to scrape down sides as needed. Beat in chocolate mini-morsels. (Mixture will be thick.) Spoon batter into prepared pan.

4. Bake at 350° for 50 to 55 minutes or until a long wooden pick inserted in center comes out clean. Cool in pan on a wire rack 10 minutes; remove from pan to wire rack, and cool completely (about 1 hour). Drizzle with Powdered Sugar Glaze.

Powdered Sugar Glaze

Mix together 1 cup powdered sugar, 4 Tbsp. heavy cream, and ½ tsp. vanilla extract to desired consistency. Makes 1 cup.

Mexican Chocolate Pound Cake

MAKES: 16 SERVINGS · **HANDS-ON:** 20 MIN. · **TOTAL:** 3 HOURS, 14 MIN., INCLUDING SAUCE

We replicated the flavor profile of Mexican chocolate using semisweet chocolate and cinnamon. If you prefer to use Mexican chocolate, look for it with the hot drink mixes or on the Hispanic food aisle.

1. Preheat oven to 325°. Microwave chocolate baking squares in a microwave-safe bowl at HIGH 1 minute and 15 seconds or until chocolate is melted and smooth, stirring at 15-second intervals. Beat butter at medium speed with a heavy-duty electric stand mixer 2 minutes or until creamy. Gradually add granulated sugar, beating 5 to 7 minutes or until light and fluffy. Add eggs, 1 at a time, beating just until yellow disappears after each addition. Stir in melted chocolate, chocolate syrup, and vanilla until smooth.

2. Combine flour and next 3 ingredients; add to butter mixture alternately with buttermilk, beginning and ending with flour mixture. Beat at low speed just until blended after each addition. Pour batter into a greased (with shortening) and floured 10-inch (16-cup) tube pan.

3. Bake at 325° for 1 hour and 10 minutes or until a long wooden pick inserted in center comes out clean. Cool in pan on a wire rack 10 to 15 minutes; remove from pan to wire rack, and let cool completely (about 1 hour and 30 minutes). Sprinkle with powdered sugar, if desired. Serve with Mexican Chocolate Sauce.

*2 (4.4-oz.) packages Mexican chocolate, chopped, may be substituted. Omit ground cinnamon.

NOTE: *We tested with Nestlé Abuelita Marqueta Mexican chocolate.*

Mexican Chocolate Sauce

Cook 8 oz. chopped semisweet chocolate baking squares, ¾ cup whipping cream, 2 tsp. light brown sugar, ¼ tsp. ground cinnamon, ¼ tsp. almond extract, and a pinch of table salt in a small saucepan over low heat, whisking occasionally, 3 to 4 minutes or until mixture is smooth and chocolate is melted. Remove from heat. Whisk in 1 Tbsp. butter until melted. Serve immediately. Makes about 1½ cups.

INGREDIENTS

1 (8-oz.) package semisweet chocolate baking squares, chopped*

1 cup butter, softened

1½ cups granulated sugar

4 large eggs

½ cup chocolate syrup

2 tsp. vanilla extract

2½ cups all-purpose flour

1 tsp. ground cinnamon

¼ tsp. baking soda

⅛ tsp. table salt

1 cup buttermilk

Shortening

Powdered sugar (optional)

Mexican Chocolate Sauce

Garnish: toasted sliced almonds

1½ cups butter, softened

3 cups sugar

5 large eggs

3 ripe bananas, mashed

3 Tbsp. milk

2 tsp. vanilla extract

3 cups all-purpose flour

1 tsp. baking powder

½ tsp. table salt

Shortening

¾ cup chopped pecans

Banana Pound Cake

MAKES: 10 TO 12 SERVINGS · **HANDS-ON:** 18 MIN. · **TOTAL:** 2 HOURS, 48 MIN.

This moist, full-flavored banana cake needs no ice cream or sauce to enhance its appeal. But if you insist, we recommend pralines-and-cream ice cream.

1. Preheat oven to 350°. Beat butter at medium speed with an electric mixer about 2 minutes or until creamy. Gradually add sugar, beating 5 to 7 minutes. Add eggs, 1 at a time, beating just until yellow disappears after each addition.

2. Combine mashed bananas, milk, and vanilla.

3. Combine flour, baking powder, and salt; add to batter alternately with banana mixture, beginning and ending with flour mixture. Beat at low speed just until blended after each addition. Pour into a greased (with shortening) and floured 10-inch (16-cup) tube pan. Sprinkle with pecans.

4. Bake at 350° for 1 hour and 20 minutes or until a long wooden pick inserted in center comes out clean. Let cool in pan on a wire rack 10 to 15 minutes. Remove from pan to wire rack, and cool completely (about 1 hour).

Serving Secret

Serve this simple-to-make cake on a white or pastel pedestal; be sure to serve it pecan-side up. Or, cut slices ahead and serve them displayed on a silver tray.

Banana Split Cake

MAKES: 10 TO 12 SERVINGS · **HANDS-ON:** 30 MIN. · **TOTAL:** 2 HOURS, 40 MIN.

1. Preheat oven to 350°. Combine first 4 ingredients in a large bowl. Stir together eggs, oil, and buttermilk. Add oil mixture to flour mixture, stirring just until dry ingredients are moistened. Stir in banana and next 3 ingredients.

2. Drain pineapple, reserving 2 Tbsp. liquid. Gently press pineapple and maraschino cherries between layers of paper towels. Chop cherries. Stir pineapple and cherries into banana mixture. Spoon into a greased (with shortening) and floured 10-inch (16-cup) tube pan.

3. Bake at 350° for 1 hour or until a long wooden pick inserted in center comes out clean. Let cool in pan on a wire rack 10 to 15 minutes. Remove from pan to wire rack, and cool completely (about 1 hour).

4. Beat cream cheese at medium speed with an electric mixer until smooth. Gradually add powdered sugar, beating at low speed until blended. Stir in reserved pineapple juice. Pour over cake.

Serving Secret

Loads of garnishes really turn this cake into a special treat fit for a party. Go all the way, or keep it simple with just one or two favorite adornments.

INGREDIENTS

3 cups all-purpose flour

2 cups sugar

1 tsp. baking soda

¼ tsp. table salt

3 large eggs

1 cup vegetable oil

½ cup buttermilk

2 cups mashed banana
(5 medium)

1 cup chopped pecans

1 cup sweetened flaked coconut

1½ tsp. vanilla extract

1 (20-oz.) can crushed
pineapple, undrained

1 (16-oz.) jar maraschino
cherries, drained

Shortening

1 (8-oz.) package cream cheese,
softened

1½ cups powdered sugar

Garnishes: grated milk
chocolate, chopped pecans,
hot fudge sauce, maraschino
cherries with stems, toasted
sweetened flaked coconut

1½ cups peeled and diced
Granny Smith apples

2 Tbsp. butter, melted

½ cup finely chopped
sweetened dried cranberries

½ cup firmly packed light
brown sugar

3 Tbsp. all-purpose flour

¾ cup finely chopped
toasted pecans

2 cups granulated sugar

1 cup butter, softened

4 large eggs

1 (15-oz.) can pumpkin

1 Tbsp. vanilla extract

3 cups all-purpose flour

2 tsp. baking powder

2 tsp. pumpkin pie spice

½ tsp. baking soda

Shortening

Maple Glaze

Sugared Pecans and Pepitas

Cranberry-Apple-Pumpkin Bundt

MAKES: 12 SERVINGS · **HANDS-ON:** 30 MIN. · **TOTAL:** 4 HOURS, 30 MIN.

1. Preheat oven to 325°. Toss diced apples in 2 Tbsp. melted butter to coat in a medium bowl; add cranberries and next 3 ingredients, and toss until well blended.

2. Beat granulated sugar and 1 cup butter at medium speed with an electric mixer until light and fluffy. Add eggs, 1 at a time, beating just until blended after each addition. Add pumpkin and vanilla; beat just until blended.

3. Stir together 3 cups flour and next 3 ingredients. Gradually add flour mixture to butter mixture, beating at low speed just until blended after each addition. Spoon half of batter into a greased (with shortening) and floured 10-inch (12-cup) Bundt pan. Spoon apple mixture over batter, leaving a ½-inch border around outer edge. Spoon remaining batter over apple mixture.

4. Bake at 325° for 1 hour and 10 minutes to 1 hour and 20 minutes or until a long wooden pick inserted in center comes out clean. Cool in pan on a wire rack 15 minutes. Remove from pan to wire rack; cool completely (about 2 hours).

5. Spoon Maple Glaze onto cooled cake. Arrange Sugared Pecans and Pepitas on cake.

Maple Glaze

Bring ½ cup pure maple syrup, 2 Tbsp. butter, and 1 Tbsp. milk to a boil in a small saucepan over medium-high heat, stirring constantly; boil, stirring constantly, 2 minutes. Remove from heat; whisk in 1 tsp. vanilla extract. Gradually whisk in 1 cup powdered sugar until smooth; stir gently 3 to 5 minutes or until mixture begins to thicken and cool slightly. Use immediately. Makes about 1 cup.

Sugared Pecans and Pepitas

Preheat oven to 350°. Stir together 1 cup pecan halves and pieces; ½ cup roasted, salted, shelled pepitas (pumpkin seeds); and 2 Tbsp. melted butter. Spread in a single layer in a 13- x 9-inch pan. Bake 12 to 15 minutes or until toasted, stirring halfway through. Remove from oven; toss with 2 Tbsp. sugar. Cool completely in pan on a wire rack. Makes 1½ cups.

Apple-Cream Cheese Bundt Cake

MAKES: 12 SERVINGS · **HANDS-ON:** 40 MIN. · **TOTAL:** 4 HOURS, 10 MIN.

This apple-laced cake features a surprise creamy filling and a praline frosting crown.

1. Preheat oven to 350°. Stir together 3 cups flour and next 7 ingredients in a large bowl; stir in eggs and next 3 ingredients, stirring just until dry ingredients are moistened. Stir in apples and pecans.

2. Spoon two-thirds of apple mixture into a greased (with shortening) and floured 10-inch (12-cup) Bundt pan. Spoon Cream Cheese Filling over apple mixture, leaving a 1-inch border around edges of pan. Swirl filling through apple mixture using a paring knife. Spoon remaining apple mixture over filling.

3. Bake at 350° for 1 hour to 1 hour and 15 minutes or until a long wooden pick inserted in center comes out clean. Cool cake in pan on a wire rack 15 minutes; remove from pan to wire rack, and cool completely (about 2 hours).

4. As soon as Praline Frosting is made, pour immediately over cooled cake.

Cream Cheese Filling

Beat 1 (8-oz.) package softened cream cheese, ¼ cup softened butter, and ½ cup granulated sugar at medium speed with an electric mixer until blended and smooth. Add 1 large egg, 2 Tbsp. all-purpose flour, and 1 tsp. vanilla extract; beat just until blended.

Praline Frosting

Bring ½ cup firmly packed brown sugar, ¼ cup butter, and 3 Tbsp. milk to a boil in a 2-qt. saucepan over medium heat, whisking constantly; boil 1 minute, whisking constantly. Remove from heat; stir in 1 tsp. vanilla extract. Gradually whisk in 1 cup powdered sugar until smooth; stir gently 3 to 5 minutes or until mixture begins to cool and thickens slightly. Use immediately.

INGREDIENTS

3 cups all-purpose flour

1 cup granulated sugar

1 cup firmly packed light brown sugar

2 tsp. ground cinnamon

1 tsp. table salt

1 tsp. baking soda

1 tsp. ground nutmeg

½ tsp. ground allspice

3 large eggs, lightly beaten

¾ cup canola oil

¾ cup applesauce

1 tsp. vanilla extract

3 cups peeled and finely chopped Gala apples (about 1½ lb.)

1 cup finely chopped toasted pecans

Shortening

Cream Cheese Filling

Praline Frosting

Garnish: chopped toasted pecans

INGREDIENTS

½ cup butter, softened

1⅓ cups granulated sugar

3 large eggs

1½ cups all-purpose flour

½ tsp. table salt

⅛ tsp. baking soda

½ cup sour cream

2 tsp. lemon zest

½ cup sweetened flaked coconut

Shortening

Poured Lemon Frosting

Garnish: Coconut Curls, lemon peel strips

Lemon-Coconut Loaf Cake

MAKES: 8 TO 10 SERVINGS • **HANDS-ON:** 30 MIN. • **TOTAL:** 2 HOURS, 35 MIN.

Garnish this pound cake with flaked coconut or, for a dressier look, curly shavings of fresh coconut.

1. Preheat oven to 325°. Beat butter at medium speed with a heavy-duty electric stand mixer until creamy. Gradually add sugar, beating until light and fluffy. Add eggs, 1 at a time, beating just until blended after each addition.

2. Stir together flour, salt, and baking soda. Add to butter mixture alternately with sour cream, beginning and ending with flour mixture. Beat at low speed just until blended after each addition. Stir in lemon zest and ½ cup coconut. Pour batter into a greased (with shortening) and floured 9- x 5-inch loaf pan.

3. Bake at 325° for 1 hour and 5 minutes to 1 hour and 10 minutes or until a long wooden pick inserted in center comes out clean. Cool in pan on a wire rack 10 to 15 minutes; remove from pan to wire rack, and cool completely (about 1 hour).

4. Spoon Poured Lemon Frosting over cake and sprinkle with Coconut Curls and lemon peel strips.

Poured Lemon Frosting

Whisk together 2 cups powdered sugar, ¾ tsp. lemon zest, and 2 Tbsp. fresh lemon juice, 1 tsp. at a time, for desired consistency. Makes about 1 cup.

Coconut Curls

Pierce 2 coconut eyes with an ice pick and hammer; drain and discard liquid. Place coconut in a 9-inch cake pan. Bake at 350° for 25 minutes or until shell begins to crack; cool 10 minutes. Break open the outer shell with a hammer, and split coconut into several large pieces. Separate coconut meat from the shell using a sturdy, blunt-ended knife, and rinse in cold water. Cut thin strips from the meat using a vegetable peeler. Use immediately, or layer between damp paper towels in an airtight container, and chill up to 2 days.

Glazed Lemon-Pear Cake

MAKES: 16 SERVINGS • **HANDS-ON:** 20 MIN. • **TOTAL:** 2 HOURS, 30 MIN.

1. Preheat oven to 350°. Grease a 10-inch (12-cup) Bundt pan with shortening (do not use cooking spray); lightly flour.

2. Combine flour, baking powder, allspice, and salt in a medium bowl; set aside. Beat butter and sugar at low speed with an electric mixer 30 seconds, scraping down sides as needed. Beat at high speed 3 minutes, scraping down sides as needed, until light and fluffy. Add eggs, 1 at a time, beating well after each addition. Add flour mixture alternately with milk, beating at low speed just until blended after each addition. Fold in pears, walnuts, and lemon zest. Pour batter into pan.

3. Bake at 350° for 1 hour or until a long wooden pick inserted in center comes out clean. Cool in pan on a wire rack 10 to 15 minutes; remove from pan to wire rack, and cool completely (about 1 hour). Spoon Poured Lemon Frosting over cake, allowing some to drizzle down sides.

Serving Secret

This delicately flavored cake is best presented whole, because the crumb is so tender. Serve cake along with a cup of hot tea for the perfect afternoon gathering.

INGREDIENTS

Shortening

3¾ cups all-purpose flour

3 tsp. baking powder

½ tsp. ground allspice

¼ tsp. table salt

1¼ cups butter, softened

1¾ cups sugar

5 large eggs

1¼ cups milk

1 cup shredded peeled pears

1 cup finely chopped toasted walnuts

¾ tsp. grated lemon zest

Poured Lemon Frosting (page 194)

1 cup butter, softened

½ cup shortening

3 cups sugar

6 large eggs

3 cups all-purpose flour

½ tsp. baking powder

⅛ tsp. table salt

1 cup milk

1 Tbsp. lemon zest

1 tsp. vanilla extract

1 tsp. lemon extract

Shortening

Lemon Curd Glaze

Garnish: lemon zest

Lemon Curd Pound Cake

MAKES: 12 SERVINGS • **HANDS-ON:** 20 MIN. • **TOTAL:** 2 HOURS, 45 MIN.

1. Preheat oven to 325°. Beat first 2 ingredients at medium speed with a heavy-duty electric stand mixer until creamy. Gradually add sugar, beating at medium speed until light and fluffy. Add eggs, 1 at a time, beating just until yellow disappears.

2. Sift together flour and next 2 ingredients; add to butter mixture alternately with milk, beginning and ending with flour mixture. Beat at low speed just until blended after each addition. Stir in lemon zest and next 2 ingredients.

3. Pour batter into a greased (with shortening) and floured 10-inch (16-cup) tube pan.

4. Bake at 325° for 1 hour and 15 minutes to 1 hour and 30 minutes or until a long wooden pick inserted in center comes out clean. Cool cake in pan on a wire rack 15 minutes.

5. Remove cake from pan to wire rack; gently spoon warm Lemon Curd Glaze over top, allowing glaze to drip down sides of cake. Cool completely on wire rack (about 1 hour).

Lemon Curd Glaze

Stir together ⅔ cup sugar, 1½ Tbsp. melted butter, 2 tsp. lemon zest, and 2 Tbsp. fresh lemon juice in a small heavy saucepan; add 1 large lightly beaten egg, and stir until blended. Cook over low heat, stirring constantly, 10 to 12 minutes or until mixture thickens slightly and begins to bubble around the edges. (Cooked mixture will have a thickness similar to heavy cream.) Use immediately. Makes ¾ cup.

Technique Tip

Wait to prepare the Lemon Curd Glaze until the cake comes out of the oven so it will still be warm when spread over the cake.

Strawberry Swirl Cream Cheese Pound Cake

MAKES: 12 SERVINGS · **HANDS-ON:** 25 MIN. · **TOTAL:** 2 HOURS, 35 MIN.

This pretty cake gets its ruby red swirl from a purchased strawberry glaze sandwiched in between layers of batter.

1. Preheat oven to 350°. Beat butter at medium speed with a heavy-duty electric stand mixer until creamy. Gradually add sugar, beating at medium speed until light and fluffy. Add cream cheese, beating until creamy. Add eggs, 1 at a time, beating just until blended after each addition.

2. Gradually add flour to butter mixture. Beat at low speed just until blended after each addition, stopping to scrape bowl as needed. Stir in almond and vanilla extracts. Pour one-third of batter into a greased (with shortening) and floured 10-inch (16-cup) tube pan (about 2⅔ cups batter). Dollop 8 rounded teaspoonfuls strawberry glaze over batter, and swirl with wooden skewer. Repeat procedure once, and top with remaining third of batter.

3. Bake at 350° for 1 hour to 1 hour and 10 minutes or until a long wooden pick inserted in center comes out clean. Cool in pan on a wire rack 10 to 15 minutes; remove from pan to wire rack, and cool completely (about 1 hour).

NOTE: *We tested with Marzetti Glaze for Strawberries.*

Quick Bite

Serve this cake piled high with fresh strawberries from your garden or farmers' market. Look for berries with stems and leaves intact for the prettiest presentation.

INGREDIENTS

1½ cups butter, softened

3 cups sugar

1 (8-oz.) package cream cheese, softened

6 large eggs

3 cups all-purpose flour

1 tsp. almond extract

½ tsp. vanilla extract

Shortening

⅔ cup strawberry glaze

1 (6-inch) wooden skewer

Garnish: fresh strawberries and leaves

INGREDIENTS

2 cups finely chopped toasted pecans, divided

2 cups butter, softened

3 cups sugar

6 large eggs

4 cups all-purpose flour

⅛ tsp. table salt

¾ cup milk

2 Tbsp. orange zest

2 tsp. ground cinnamon

1 tsp. ground nutmeg

1 tsp. vanilla extract

1 tsp. lemon extract

1 tsp. orange extract

½ tsp. ground cloves

Orange Syrup

Garnishes: pecan halves, halved orange slices

Orange-Pecan-Spice Pound Cake

MAKES: 10 TO 12 SERVINGS · **HANDS-ON:** 35 MIN. · **TOTAL:** 3 HOURS, 35 MIN.

Sprinkle chopped pecans into the buttered tube pan before spooning in the batter to form a nice, crisp coating for the top of this pound cake.

1. Preheat oven to 300°. Sprinkle 1¼ cups toasted pecans into a generously buttered 10-inch (16-cup) tube pan; shake to evenly coat bottom and sides of pan.

2. Beat 2 cups butter at medium speed with an electric mixer until creamy; gradually add sugar, beating well. Add eggs, 1 at a time, beating until blended after each addition.

3. Combine flour and salt; add to butter mixture alternately with milk, beginning and ending with flour mixture. Beat at low speed until blended after each addition. Stir in orange zest, next 6 ingredients, and remaining ¾ cup pecans. Spoon batter into prepared pan.

4. Bake at 300° for 1 hour and 30 minutes to 1 hour and 40 minutes or until a long wooden pick inserted in center comes out clean. Let cool in pan on a wire rack 20 minutes. Remove cake from pan; invert cake, pecan crust side up, onto wire rack.

5. Brush top and sides of pound cake gently several times with hot Orange Syrup, allowing the cake to absorb the Orange Syrup after each brushing. (Do not pour syrup over the cake.) Let cake cool completely (about 1 hour).

Orange Syrup

Remove zest from 1 large orange with a vegetable peeler, being careful not to get the bitter white pith. Set orange zest aside. Squeeze orange to get ½ cup juice. Combine orange zest, juice, and 1 cup sugar in a small saucepan. Cook over low heat, stirring until sugar dissolves. Bring mixture to a boil over medium-high heat, and boil 2 minutes. Makes 1 cup.

Green Tea-Honeysuckle Cake

MAKES: 12 SERVINGS · **HANDS-ON:** 30 MIN. · **TOTAL:** 3 HOURS, 15 MIN.

Matcha, a Japanese green tea powder, adds vivid green color and a delicate flavor. Look for it in Asian grocery stores and gourmet markets, or order it online. Store it tightly covered in the fridge. If you can't find matcha, pulverize regular green tea in a spice grinder.

1. Preheat oven to 325°. Beat butter and shortening at medium speed with a heavy-duty electric stand mixer until creamy. Gradually add sugar, beating until light and fluffy. Add honey, beating until blended. Add eggs, 1 at a time, beating just until blended after each addition.

2. Stir together flour and next 2 ingredients. Add to butter mixture alternately with milk, beginning and ending with flour mixture. Beat at low speed just until blended after each addition. Transfer 2½ cups batter to a 2-qt. bowl, and stir in matcha until blended.

3. Drop 2 scoops of plain batter into a greased (with shortening) and floured 10-inch (12-cup) Bundt pan, using a small cookie scoop (about 1½ inches); top with 1 scoop of matcha batter. Repeat procedure around entire pan, covering bottom completely. Continue layering batters in pan as directed until all batter is used.

4. Bake at 325° for 1 hour and 5 minutes to 1 hour and 15 minutes or until a long wooden pick inserted in center comes out clean.

5. Remove cake from oven, and gradually spoon 1 cup hot Honeysuckle Glaze over cake in pan, allowing glaze to soak into cake after each addition. Reserve remaining glaze. Cool cake completely in pan on a wire rack (about 1 hour and 30 minutes). Remove cake from pan; spoon reserved glaze over cake.

Honeysuckle Glaze

Bring ¾ cup sugar, ½ cup butter, ⅓ cup honey, ⅓ cup orange liqueur, and 3 Tbsp. water to a boil in a 1-qt. saucepan over medium heat, stirring often; reduce heat to medium-low, and boil, stirring constantly, 3 minutes. Makes about 1⅔ cups.

INGREDIENTS

1 cup butter, softened

½ cup shortening

2½ cups sugar

¼ cup honey

6 large eggs

3 cups all-purpose flour

1 tsp. baking powder

½ tsp. table salt

¾ cup milk

2 tsp. matcha (green tea powder)

Shortening

Honeysuckle Glaze

1½ cups chopped black walnuts

1 cup butter, softened

1½ cups granulated sugar

3 large eggs, separated

1 tsp. vanilla extract

2 cups all-purpose flour

1 Tbsp. baking powder

¼ tsp. table salt

¾ cup milk

Shortening

¼ cup powdered sugar

Vanilla ice cream (optional)

Sliced fresh strawberries (optional)

Chopped black walnuts (optional)

Maryland Black Walnut Cake

MAKES: 12 SERVINGS · **HANDS-ON:** 20 MIN. · **TOTAL:** 2 HOURS, 30 MIN.

Black walnut trees are native to Maryland and much of the eastern United States. A black sheep of the tree world, they are toxic to some other landscape plants and messy when in leaf. But their wood is prized for furniture and cabinets, and their notoriously difficult-to-crack nuts have a rich, distinctive flavor beloved by local bakers and others who've acquired a taste for them.

1. Preheat oven to 350°. Pulse black walnuts in a food processor 8 to 10 times or until finely ground; set aside.

2. Beat butter at medium speed with an electric mixer until creamy; gradually add granulated sugar, beating until light and fluffy. Add egg yolks and vanilla, beating just until blended.

3. Sift together flour, baking powder, and salt; add to butter mixture alternately with milk, beginning and ending with flour mixture. Beat batter at low speed just until blended after each addition.

4. Beat egg whites at medium speed with an electric mixer until stiff peaks form; fold into batter. Fold ground walnuts into batter. Spoon batter evenly into a greased (with shortening) and floured 10-inch (12-cup) Bundt pan.

5. Bake at 350° for 50 minutes or until a long wooden pick inserted in center comes out clean. Cool in pan on a wire rack 10 to 15 minutes; remove from pan to wire rack, and cool completely (about 1 hour). Sprinkle evenly with powdered sugar. Serve with vanilla ice cream, sliced fresh strawberries, and walnuts, if desired.

Coffee Cake Pound Cake

MAKES: 12 SERVINGS · **HANDS-ON:** 30 MIN. · **TOTAL:** 3 HOURS

This year, resolve to think beyond a ho-hum box of chocolates for a hostess gift. Instead, pass along this sweet treat, which marries two Southern specialties, coffee cake and pound cake, to create one tender, buttery, best-of-both-worlds dessert.

1. Preheat oven to 325°. Beat butter at medium speed with a heavy-duty electric stand mixer until creamy. Gradually add granulated sugar, beating until light and fluffy. Add eggs, 1 at a time, beating just until blended after each addition.

2. Stir together flour and baking soda; add to butter mixture alternately with sour cream, beginning and ending with flour mixture. Beat at low speed just until blended after each addition. Stir in vanilla.

3. Pour half of batter into a greased (with shortening) and floured 10-inch (16-cup) tube pan. Stir together toasted pecans, brown sugar, and cinnamon; sprinkle over batter. Spoon remaining batter over pecan mixture; sprinkle with Pecan Streusel.

4. Bake at 325° for 1 hour and 20 minutes to 1 hour and 30 minutes or until a long wooden pick inserted in center comes out clean. Cool in pan on a wire rack 10 to 15 minutes; remove from pan to wire rack, and cool completely (about 1 hour).

Pecan Streusel

Combine ½ cup firmly packed brown sugar, ½ cup all-purpose flour, and 1 tsp. ground cinnamon in a bowl. Cut in ¼ cup butter with a pastry blender until crumbly. Stir in ¾ cup chopped pecans.

INGREDIENTS

1 cup butter, softened

2½ cups granulated sugar

6 large eggs

3 cups all-purpose flour

¼ tsp. baking soda

1 (8-oz.) container sour cream

2 tsp. vanilla extract

Shortening

1 cup finely chopped toasted pecans

¼ cup firmly packed brown sugar

1½ tsp. ground cinnamon

Pecan Streusel

¾ cup milk

1 (2.7-oz.) jar crystallized ginger, finely minced

2 cups butter, softened

3 cups sugar

6 large eggs

4 cups all-purpose flour

1 tsp. vanilla extract

Shortening

Vanilla bean ice cream

Garnish: chopped crystallized ginger

Ginger Pound Cake

MAKES: 10 TO 12 SERVINGS • **HANDS-ON:** 25 MIN. • **TOTAL:** 3 HOURS, 20 MIN.

1. Preheat oven to 325°. Cook milk and ginger in a saucepan over medium heat 5 minutes or until thoroughly heated (do not boil). Remove from heat, and let stand 10 to 15 minutes.

2. Beat butter at medium speed with an electric mixer until creamy; gradually add sugar, beating 5 to 7 minutes. Add eggs, 1 at a time, beating just until yellow disappears after each addition.

3. Add flour to butter mixture alternately with milk mixture, beginning and ending with flour. Beat at low speed just until blended after each addition. Stir in vanilla. Pour batter into a greased (with shortening) and floured 10-inch (16-cup) tube pan.

4. Bake at 325° for 1 hour and 25 minutes or until a long wooden pick inserted in center comes out clean. Cool in pan on a wire rack 10 to 15 minutes; remove from pan to wire rack, and cool completely (about 1 hour). Serve with ice cream.

Technique Tip

By simmering the ginger pieces in with the milk, the milk is not only infused with ginger flavor, but the crystallized pieces are softened so they will be more easily incorporated into the batter.

Rosemary-Olive Oil Cornmeal Cake

MAKES: 16 SERVINGS · **HANDS-ON:** 15 MIN. · **TOTAL:** 3 HOURS

1. Preheat oven to 325°. Generously grease a 10-inch (12-cup) Bundt pan with shortening; lightly flour.

2. Combine flour, cornmeal, and salt in a medium bowl; set aside. Beat granulated sugar and butter at medium speed with an electric mixer 2 minutes or until light and fluffy. Gradually add oil, beating just until blended. Add rosemary, orange zest, and vanilla. Beat in eggs, 1 at a time, until blended. Gradually beat in flour mixture at low speed just until blended. Pour batter into prepared pan.

3. Bake at 325° for 1 hour and 10 minutes to 1 hour and 15 minutes or until a long wooden pick inserted in center comes out clean. Cool in pan on a wire rack 10 to 15 minutes; remove from pan to wire rack, and cool completely (about 1 hour). Sprinkle with powdered sugar before serving, if desired.

Quick Bite

Be sure to use a good-quality extra virgin olive oil for this recipe; the fruity flavor of the olive oil marries beautifully with the fresh rosemary.

INGREDIENTS

Shortening

2½ cups all-purpose flour

1 cup plain yellow cornmeal

½ tsp. table salt

2½ cups granulated sugar

¾ cup butter (do not use margarine), softened

¾ cup extra virgin olive oil

1 Tbsp. chopped fresh rosemary leaves

2 tsp. orange zest

1 tsp. vanilla extract

6 large eggs

Garnish: powdered sugar

INGREDIENTS

1 cup butter, softened

½ cup shortening

1 (16-oz.) package light
brown sugar

5 large eggs

1 (5-oz.) can evaporated milk

½ cup bourbon

3 cups all-purpose flour

½ tsp. baking powder

½ tsp. table salt

1 Tbsp. vanilla bean paste

Shortening

2 Tbsp. powdered sugar

Garnishes: candied oranges,
magnolia leaves

Brown Sugar-
Bourbon Bundt

MAKES: 12 SERVINGS · **HANDS-ON:** 20 MIN. · **TOTAL:** 2 HOURS, 35 MIN.

1. Preheat oven to 325°. Beat butter and shortening at medium speed with a heavy-duty electric stand mixer until creamy. Gradually add brown sugar, beating at medium speed until light and creamy. Add eggs, 1 at a time, beating just until blended after each addition.

2. Stir together evaporated milk and bourbon in a bowl. Stir together flour, baking powder, and salt in another bowl. Add flour mixture to butter mixture alternately with milk mixture, beginning and ending with flour mixture. Beat at low speed just until blended after each addition. Stir in vanilla bean paste. Pour batter into a greased (with shortening) and floured 10-inch (12-cup) Bundt pan.

3. Bake at 325° for 1 hour and 5 minutes to 1 hour and 10 minutes or until a long wooden pick inserted in center comes out clean. Cool in pan on a wire rack 10 to 15 minutes; remove from pan to wire rack. Cool completely (about 1 hour). Dust top lightly with powdered sugar.

Technique Tip

To get this intricate fluted look or other design to your cake, look for an ornate Bundt pan. There are so many styles on the market—you can't go wrong!

Amaretto-Almond Pound Cake

MAKES: 12 SERVINGS · **HANDS-ON:** 20 MIN. · **TOTAL:** 3 HOURS

1. Preheat oven to 325°. Sprinkle almonds over bottom of a greased (with shortening) and floured 10-inch (12-cup) Bundt pan.

2. Beat butter and cream cheese at medium speed with a heavy-duty electric stand mixer until creamy. Gradually add sugar, beating at medium speed until light and fluffy. Add liqueur and vanilla, beating just until blended. Gradually add flour to butter mixture, beating at low speed just until blended after each addition. Add eggs, 1 at a time, beating at low speed just until blended after each addition. Pour batter over almonds in prepared pan.

3. Bake at 325° for 1 hour and 5 minutes to 1 hour and 10 minutes or until a long wooden pick inserted in center comes out clean.

4. Gradually spoon hot Amaretto Glaze over cake, allowing it to soak into cake after each addition. Cool completely in pan on a wire rack (about 1 hour and 30 minutes).

Amaretto Glaze

Mix ¾ cup sugar, 6 Tbsp. butter, ¼ cup amaretto, and 2 Tbsp. water in a 1-qt. saucepan. Heat to boiling over medium heat, stirring often. Reduce heat to medium-low; cook 3 minutes, stirring constantly. Makes about 1 cup.

Quick Bite

The rich flavor of amaretto pairs perfectly with sliced almonds in this cake. The principal ingredient in amaretto is apricot kernels, which impart the same flavor as almond extract.

INGREDIENTS

⅓ cup sliced almonds

Shortening

1¼ cups butter, softened

1 (3-oz.) package cream cheese, softened

2½ cups sugar

3 Tbsp. amaretto liqueur

1 Tbsp. vanilla extract

2½ cups all-purpose flour

6 large eggs

Amaretto Glaze

INGREDIENTS

1 cup butter, softened

3 cups sugar, divided

6 large eggs, separated

3 cups all-purpose flour

¼ tsp. baking soda

1 (8-oz.) container sour cream

1 tsp. vanilla extract

1 tsp. lemon extract

Shortening

Buttered Rum Glaze

Bananas Foster Sauce

Garnish: chopped toasted pecans

Buttered Rum Pound Cake with Bananas Foster Sauce

MAKES: 10 TO 12 SERVINGS · **HANDS-ON:** 29 MIN. · **TOTAL:** 5 HOURS, 40 MIN.

1. Preheat oven to 325°. Beat butter at medium speed with a heavy-duty electric stand mixer until creamy. Add 2½ cups sugar, beating 4 to 5 minutes or until fluffy. Add egg yolks, 1 at a time, beating just until yellow disappears after each addition.

2. Combine flour and baking soda; add to butter mixture alternately with sour cream, beginning and ending with flour mixture. Beat at medium speed just until blended after each addition. Stir in extracts.

3. Beat egg whites until foamy; gradually add remaining ½ cup sugar, 1 Tbsp. at a time, beating until stiff peaks form. Fold into batter. Pour batter into a greased (with shortening) and floured 10-inch (16-cup) tube pan.

4. Bake at 325° for 1 hour and 30 minutes or until a long wooden pick inserted in center comes out clean. Let cool in pan 10 to 15 minutes. Remove from pan, and place on a serving plate. While warm, prick cake surface at 1-inch intervals with a wooden pick; spoon warm Buttered Rum Glaze over cake. Let stand, covered, at least 4 hours or overnight. Serve with Bananas Foster Sauce.

Buttered Rum Glaze

Combine 6 Tbsp. butter, 3 Tbsp. light rum, ¾ cup sugar, and 3 Tbsp. water in a small saucepan; bring to a boil. Boil, stirring constantly, 3 minutes. Remove from heat, and stir in ½ cup chopped toasted pecans. Makes 1¼ cups.

Bananas Foster Sauce

Melt ¼ cup butter in a large skillet over medium heat; add ½ cup firmly packed brown sugar, ⅓ cup banana liqueur, and ¼ tsp. ground cinnamon. Cook, stirring constantly, 3 minutes or until bubbly. Add 4 peeled and sliced bananas, and cook 2 to 3 minutes or until thoroughly heated. Remove from heat. Pour ⅓ cup light rum over banana mixture, and carefully ignite the fumes above the mixture with a long match or multipurpose lighter. Let flames die down; serve immediately. Makes 2½ cups.

Rum Cake

MAKES: 10 TO 12 SERVINGS · **HANDS-ON:** 20 MIN. · **TOTAL:** 2 HOURS, 20 MIN.

This moist, rich rum cake is great to make ahead for special occasions or as a food gift. It tastes even better the next day, as the Banana-Rum Syrup soaks in.

1. Preheat oven to 350°. Beat butter and granulated sugar at medium speed with an electric mixer until light and fluffy. Add eggs, egg yolk, and vanilla, beating until blended. Add lemon zest, beating until blended. Gradually add rum and banana liqueur, beating until blended. (Batter will look curdled.)

2. Stir together flour and next 3 ingredients; add to butter mixture alternately with whipping cream, beginning and ending with flour mixture. Beat batter at low speed just until blended after each addition. Pour batter into a greased (with shortening) and floured 10-inch (12-cup) Bundt pan.

3. Bake at 350° for 55 to 60 minutes or until a long wooden pick inserted in center comes out clean.

4. Cool in pan on a wire rack 15 minutes. Pierce cake multiple times using a long wooden pick. Pour Banana-Rum Syrup evenly over cake. Let stand 45 minutes. Remove from pan; cool completely on a wire rack. Sprinkle evenly with powdered sugar before serving.

Banana-Rum Syrup

Melt 10 Tbsp. butter in a 2-qt. saucepan over medium-high heat; stir in ¾ cup sugar, ¼ cup dark rum, and ¼ cup banana liqueur. Bring to a boil, stirring often; reduce heat to low, and cook, stirring often, 8 to 10 minutes or until slightly thickened. Remove from heat, and cool 10 minutes. Makes about 1 cup.

*¼ cup dark rum may be substituted for banana liqueur.

INGREDIENTS

1½ cups butter, softened

1½ cups granulated sugar

3 large eggs

1 large egg yolk

2 tsp. vanilla extract

2 Tbsp. lemon zest

½ cup dark rum

¼ cup banana liqueur*

3 cups all-purpose flour

2 tsp. baking powder

½ tsp. baking soda

⅛ tsp. table salt

1 cup whipping cream

Shortening

Banana-Rum Syrup

Powdered sugar

CAKES
FOR A CROWD

Peanut-Cola Cake

MAKES: 12 SERVINGS · **HANDS-ON:** 20 MIN. · **TOTAL:** 1 HOUR, INCLUDING FROSTING

The South's favorite drink is a key ingredient in this moist Peanut-Cola Cake and is the reason this cake bakes up so moist and tender.

1. Preheat oven to 350°. Combine cola and buttermilk in a 2-cup measuring cup.

2. Beat butter at low speed with an electric mixer until creamy. Gradually add sugar, beating until blended. Add eggs and vanilla; beat at low speed just until blended.

3. Combine flour and next 2 ingredients in a medium bowl. Add to butter mixture alternately with cola mixture, beginning and ending with flour mixture. Beat at low speed just until blended after each addition. Lightly grease a 13- x 9-inch pan with cooking spray. Pour batter into pan.

4. Bake at 350° for 30 to 35 minutes or until a wooden pick inserted in center comes out clean. Cool in pan on a wire rack 10 minutes.

5. Meanwhile, prepare Peanut Butter Poured Icing. Pour over warm cake. Sprinkle with chopped peanuts.

Peanut Butter Poured Icing

Melt ¼ cup butter in a large saucepan over medium heat. Whisk in ¾ cup milk, and bring to a boil, whisking constantly. Reduce heat to low, and whisk in 1 cup creamy peanut butter until smooth. Gradually whisk in 1 (16-oz.) package powdered sugar until smooth; remove from heat, and whisk in 1 tsp. vanilla. Use immediately. Makes 3 cups.

Serving Secret

This homestyle cake tastes divine but isn't the prettiest. Be sure to serve it already sliced and either on some dainty dessert plates or gathered upon a pedestal.

INGREDIENTS

1 cup cola soft drink

½ cup buttermilk

1 cup butter, softened

1¾ cups sugar

2 large eggs, lightly beaten

2 tsp. vanilla extract

2 cups all-purpose flour

¼ cup unsweetened cocoa

1 tsp. baking soda

Vegetable cooking spray

Peanut Butter Poured Icing

1 cup chopped honey-roasted peanuts

INGREDIENTS

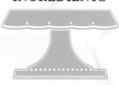

Shortening

3 cups all-purpose flour

⅓ cup unsweetened
dark baking cocoa

1½ tsp. baking soda

1 tsp. table salt

1¼ cups packed dark brown sugar

1¼ cups granulated sugar

1 cup butter, softened

4 large eggs

1 (8-oz.) package semisweet
chocolate baking squares,
melted and cooled

1½ tsp. vanilla extract

1⅔ cups buttermilk

1 cup strong brewed coffee
(room temperature)

Peanut Butter Frosting

Garnish: 12 peanut butter
cream-filled chocolate
sandwich cookies, chopped

Peanut Butter-Chocolate Cake

MAKES: 20 SERVINGS • **HANDS-ON:** 20 MIN. • **TOTAL:** 2 HOURS, 20 MIN.

1. Preheat oven to 350°. Grease (with shortening) and lightly flour a 13- x 9-inch pan.

2. Mix flour, cocoa, baking soda, and salt in a medium bowl; set aside. Beat brown sugar, granulated sugar, and 1 cup butter at medium speed with an electric mixer 2 minutes or until light and fluffy. Add eggs, 1 at a time, beating until well blended. Add melted chocolate and vanilla, beating until blended. Alternately add flour mixture and buttermilk, beginning and ending with flour mixture. Beat at low speed just until blended after each addition. Beat in coffee until blended. Pour batter into prepared pan.

3. Bake at 350° for 55 to 60 minutes or until a wooden pick inserted in center comes out clean. Cool in pan on a wire rack 10 to 15 minutes; remove from pan to wire rack, and cool completely (about 1 hour). Spread top of cake with frosting.

Peanut Butter Frosting

Beat ½ cup softened butter, ½ cup creamy peanut butter, and 2 (3-oz.) packages softened cream cheese at medium speed with an electric mixer 2 minutes or until blended. Gradually beat in 1 (16-oz.) package powdered sugar at low speed until blended. Beat in 1 Tbsp. whipping cream and 2 tsp. vanilla.

Quick Bite

This sheet cake relies on baking soda—not baking powder—to rise when baked. The acidity of the cocoa, buttermilk, and coffee all help the baking soda do its job.

226 The Southern Cake Book

Mississippi Mud Cake

MAKES: 15 SERVINGS • HANDS-ON: 15 MIN. • TOTAL: 51 MIN.

Just like the banks of the Mississippi River, this cake is ooey, gooey, and chocolate-brown. The original Mississippi mud cake is thought to have been created by World War II-era cooks who found a way to use available ingredients to make a dense chocolate cake.

1. Preheat oven to 350°. Grease (with shortening) a 15- x 10-inch jelly-roll pan.

2. Microwave 1 cup butter and chocolate bar in a large microwave-safe glass bowl at HIGH 1 minute, stirring at 30-second intervals. Whisk sugar and next 5 ingredients into chocolate mixture. Pour batter into prepared pan.

3. Bake at 350° for 20 minutes. Remove from oven, and sprinkle evenly with miniature marshmallows; bake 8 to 10 more minutes or until golden brown. Drizzle warm cake with Chocolate Frosting, and sprinkle evenly with toasted pecans.

Chocolate Frosting

Melt ½ cup butter in a saucepan over medium heat. Whisk in ⅓ cup milk and ¼ cup unsweetened cocoa, and bring mixture to a boil, whisking constantly. Remove from heat. Gradually add 1 (16-oz.) package powdered sugar, stirring until smooth; stir in 1 tsp. vanilla. Use immediately. Makes 3 cups.

Technique Tip

To thin frosting, add 1 Tbsp. milk. To serve remaining Chocolate Frosting over pound cake or ice cream, microwave frosting in a medium-size microwave-safe glass bowl at HIGH 15 seconds or until warm.

INGREDIENTS

Shortening

1 cup butter

1 (4-oz.) semisweet chocolate baking bar, chopped

2 cups sugar

1½ cups all-purpose flour

½ cup unsweetened cocoa

4 large eggs

1 tsp. vanilla extract

¾ tsp. table salt

1 (10.5-oz.) bag miniature marshmallows

Chocolate Frosting

1 cup chopped toasted pecans

INGREDIENTS

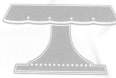

1 cup butter, softened

1¾ cups sugar, divided

2 large eggs

2 tsp. vanilla extract

2½ cups all-purpose flour

1 Tbsp. baking powder

½ tsp. table salt

1 cup half-and-half

¼ cup unsweetened cocoa

3 Tbsp. hot water

Shortening

Mocha Frosting

Chocolate Marble Sheet Cake

MAKES: 12 SERVINGS • **HANDS-ON:** 20 MIN. • **TOTAL:** 1 HOUR, 43 MIN.

This cake's rich, creamy frosting blends coffee with cocoa for a delightful mocha flavor.

1. Preheat oven to 325°. Beat butter and 1½ cups sugar at medium speed with a heavy-duty electric stand mixer 4 to 5 minutes or until creamy. Add eggs, 1 at a time, beating just until blended after each addition. Beat in vanilla.

2. Sift together flour, baking powder, and salt. Add to butter mixture alternately with half-and-half, beginning and ending with flour mixture. Beat at low speed just until blended after each addition, stopping to scrape bowl as needed.

3. Spoon 1¼ cups batter into a 2-qt. bowl, and stir in cocoa, 3 Tbsp. hot water, and remaining ¼ cup sugar until well blended.

4. Spread remaining vanilla batter into a greased (with shortening) and floured 15- x 10-inch jelly-roll pan. Spoon chocolate batter onto vanilla batter in pan; gently swirl with a knife or small spatula.

5. Bake at 325° for 23 to 28 minutes or until a wooden pick inserted in center comes out clean. Let cool completely in pan on a wire rack (about 1 hour). Spread top of cake with Mocha Frosting.

Mocha Frosting

Whisk together 3 cups powdered sugar and ⅔ cup unsweetened cocoa in a medium bowl. Combine 3 Tbsp. hot coffee and 2 tsp. vanilla. Beat ½ cup softened butter at medium speed with a heavy-duty electric stand mixer until creamy; gradually add sugar mixture alternately with coffee mixture, beating at low speed until blended. Beat in 3 to 4 Tbsp. half-and-half, 1 Tbsp. at a time, until smooth and mixture has reached desired consistency. Makes 2⅓ cups.

Lemon-Yogurt Crumb Cake

MAKES: 8 TO 10 SERVINGS • **HANDS-ON:** 30 MIN. • **TOTAL:** 5 HOURS, 35 MIN.

We love the swirls of lemon curd in this cake, but it's also delicious without it.

1. Preheat oven to 350°. Combine first 5 ingredients; cut cold butter into flour mixture with a pastry blender until crumbly. Cover and chill until ready to use.

2. Beat softened butter at medium speed with a heavy-duty electric stand mixer until creamy. Add 1¼ cups granulated sugar, beating 3 minutes or until fluffy. Add egg yolks, 1 at a time, beating just until yellow disappears. Stir together flour and baking soda; add to butter mixture alternately with yogurt, beginning and ending with flour mixture. Stir in lemon zest.

3. Beat egg whites at high speed until foamy; gradually add remaining ¼ cup granulated sugar, 1 Tbsp. at a time, beating until stiff peaks form. Fold into batter. Pour batter into a greased (with shortening) and floured 9-inch square (2-inch-deep) pan. Dollop with Quick and Easy Lemon Curd; gently swirl with a knife. Sprinkle crumb topping over batter.

4. Bake at 350° for 45 to 50 minutes or until a wooden pick inserted in center comes out clean. Remove from oven; dust with powdered sugar. Serve warm, or cool on a wire rack 1 hour.

Quick and Easy Lemon Curd

1. Grate zest from 6 lemons to equal 2 Tbsp. Cut lemons in half; squeeze juice into a measuring cup to equal 1 cup.

2. Beat ½ cup softened butter and 2 cups sugar at medium speed with an electric mixer until blended. Add 4 large eggs, 1 at a time, beating just until blended after each addition. Gradually add lemon juice to butter mixture, beating at low speed just until blended after each addition; stir in zest. (Mixture will look curdled.) Transfer to a 3-qt. microwave-safe bowl. Microwave at HIGH 5 minutes, stirring at 1-minute intervals. Microwave, stirring at 30-second intervals, 1 to 2 more minutes or until mixture thickens, coats the back of a spoon, and starts to mound slightly when stirred.

3. Place heavy-duty plastic wrap directly on warm curd (to prevent a film from forming), and chill 4 hours or until firm. Store in an airtight container in refrigerator up to 2 weeks. Makes 2 cups.

INGREDIENTS

1½ cups all-purpose flour

⅔ cup granulated sugar

1 Tbsp. lemon zest

1 Tbsp. orange zest

⅛ tsp. table salt

½ cup cold butter, cut into pieces

½ cup butter, softened

1½ cups granulated sugar, divided

3 large eggs, separated

1½ cups all-purpose flour

⅛ tsp. baking soda

½ cup plain Greek yogurt

1 Tbsp. lemon zest

Shortening

¾ cup Quick and Easy Lemon Curd

¼ cup powdered sugar

Shortening

2¾ cups all-purpose flour

1⅔ cups granulated sugar

1 cup milk

¾ cup butter, softened

½ cup presweetened pink lemonade flavor drink mix (from 19-oz. container)

3 tsp. baking powder

2 tsp. vanilla extract

1 tsp. grated lemon zest

¼ tsp. table salt

4 large egg whites

1 whole large egg

Pink Lemonade Frosting

Garnishes: pink decorating sugar, edible pink pearls

Pink Lemonade Cake

MAKES: 15 SERVINGS • **HANDS-ON:** 35 MIN. • **TOTAL:** 2 HOURS, 15 MIN.

1. Preheat oven to 350°. Grease (with shortening) and lightly flour a 13- x 9-inch pan.

2. Beat flour and next 8 ingredients at low speed with an electric mixer 30 seconds, scraping down sides as needed. Beat at high speed 2 minutes, scraping down sides as needed. Beat in egg whites and egg at high speed 2 minutes, scraping down sides as needed. Pour batter into prepared pan.

3. Bake at 350° for 35 to 45 minutes or until a wooden pick inserted in center comes out clean. Cool in pan on wire rack 10 to 15 minutes; remove from pan to wire rack, and cool completely (about 1 hour). Spread top of cake with frosting.

NOTE: *We tested with Country Time Pink Lemonade Flavor Drink Mix.*

Pink Lemonade Frosting

Stir ¼ cup presweetened pink lemonade flavor drink mix in 3 Tbsp. water until dissolved. Beat ½ cup softened butter, 1 Tbsp. whipping cream, 1 tsp. lemon zest, and lemonade mixture at low speed with an electric mixer 30 seconds or until creamy. Gradually add 1 (16-oz.) package powdered sugar, beating at low speed until blended. Gradually beat in 1 to 2 Tbsp. whipping cream, 1 tsp. at a time, to make frosting smooth and spreadable.

Quick Bite

Using a presweetened and flavored drink mix is a super-easy shortcut for adding a bunch of flavor to baked goods. For this recipe, you can substitute regular lemonade drink mix, if preferred.

Strawberry Shortcake

MAKES: 8 SERVINGS • **HANDS-ON:** 30 MIN. • **TOTAL:** 2 HOURS, 8 MIN.

Whipped cream and sliced fresh strawberries crown each layer of this delectable party-size shortcake.

1. Combine sliced strawberries and desired amount of granulated sugar; stir gently, and chill 1 to 2 hours. Drain.

2. Preheat oven to 450°. Butter 2 (9-inch) round cake pans with ½ tsp. butter each. Combine flour and next 4 ingredients in a large bowl; cut in remaining butter with a pastry blender until mixture is crumbly.

3. Whisk together milk and egg yolks. Add to flour mixture; stir with a fork until a soft dough forms. Pat dough out into prepared cake pans. (Dough will be sticky; moisten fingers with water as necessary.)

4. Beat egg whites at medium speed with an electric mixer just until stiff peaks form. Brush surface of dough with beaten egg white; sprinkle with ¼ cup granulated sugar.

5. Bake at 450° for 8 to 10 minutes or until layers are golden brown. (Layers will be thin.) Remove from pans to wire racks, and let cool completely (about 30 minutes).

6. Beat whipping cream until foamy; gradually add powdered sugar, beating until soft peaks form. Place 1 cake layer on a serving plate. Spread half of whipped cream over layer, and arrange half of sweetened strawberries on top. Repeat procedure with remaining layer, whipped cream, and sweetened strawberries, reserving a small amount of whipped cream. Top cake with remaining whipped cream. Store in refrigerator.

Serving Secret

For best results, whip cream and assemble cake just before serving. Pile whipped cream in the center of the first layer; when you add the second layer, it will press the cream outward.

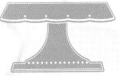

INGREDIENTS

2 (16-oz.) containers fresh strawberries, sliced

¼ to ½ cup granulated sugar

½ cup butter, softened and divided

2 cups all-purpose flour

1 Tbsp. plus 1 tsp. baking powder

¼ tsp. table salt

¼ cup granulated sugar

Dash of ground nutmeg

½ cup milk

2 large eggs, separated

¼ cup granulated sugar

1 cup whipping cream

¼ cup powdered sugar

Garnishes: sliced fresh strawberries and leaves

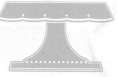

Shortening

3 cups all-purpose flour

1 tsp. baking soda

1 tsp. table salt

1 tsp. ground cinnamon

¼ tsp. ground allspice

1 cup granulated sugar

1 cup packed brown sugar

1 cup vegetable oil

2 very ripe bananas, mashed
(to equal 1 cup)

3 large eggs, beaten

1 cup flaked coconut

1 (8-oz.) can crushed pineapple,
undrained

1 (16-oz.) container cream
cheese frosting

½ cup flaked coconut, toasted

15 dried banana chips
(about ½ cup), if desired

Hawaiian Sheet Cake

MAKES: 15 SERVINGS · **HANDS-ON:** 15 MIN · **TOTAL:** 2 HOURS, 30 MIN.

1. Preheat oven to 350°. Grease (with shortening) and lightly flour a 13- x 9-inch pan.

2. Mix flour, baking soda, salt, cinnamon, and allspice in a large bowl; set aside. Mix granulated sugar, brown sugar, oil, bananas, and eggs with whisk in a medium bowl. Add to flour mixture, stirring with whisk until blended. Stir in coconut and pineapple. Pour batter into prepared pan.

3. Bake at 350° for 40 to 45 minutes or until a wooden pick inserted in center comes out clean. Cool completely in pan on a wire rack (about 1 hour and 30 minutes).

4. Spread top of cake with frosting; sprinkle with toasted coconut. Top each serving with 1 banana chip.

Technique Tip

To mash bananas for this recipe, be sure to start with very ripe bananas. You can easily crush them with clean hands, or you can use a potato masher, mashing them in a small bowl before adding to batter.

Dutch Sorghum Cake

MAKES: 2 (9-INCH) SQUARE CAKES • **HANDS-ON:** 25 MIN. • **TOTAL:** 1 HOUR, 50 MIN.

1. Preheat oven to 325°. Beat sugar and shortening at medium speed with an electric mixer until fluffy. Stop mixer, and add sorghum; beat just until blended. Add eggs, 1 at a time, beating until blended after each addition.

2. Combine flour and next 4 ingredients; gradually add to sugar mixture alternately with buttermilk, beginning and ending with flour mixture. Beat at low speed just until blended after each addition. Stir in raisins, dates, and pecans. Spoon into 2 greased (with shortening) and floured 9-inch square pans.

3. Bake at 325° for 32 to 35 minutes or until a wooden pick inserted in center comes out clean. Cool completely on a wire rack (about 45 minutes). Drizzle each cake with Coffee Glaze.

Coffee Glaze

Whisk together 1 cup powdered sugar and 1½ Tbsp. coffee in a small bowl until smooth. Makes about ⅓ cup.

Quick Bite

This recipe is super-moist and flavorful thanks to the addition of sorghum, raisins, and dates. If you're not a date lover, you can omit them and increase raisins to 2 cups.

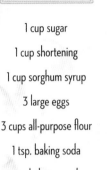

INGREDIENTS

1 cup sugar

1 cup shortening

1 cup sorghum syrup

3 large eggs

3 cups all-purpose flour

1 tsp. baking soda

1 tsp. baking powder

1 tsp. ground ginger

1 tsp. ground cinnamon

1 cup buttermilk

1 cup raisins

1 cup chopped dates

1 cup chopped toasted pecans

Shortening

Coffee Glaze

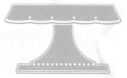

½ cup butter, melted

2 cups sugar

2 large eggs

1 tsp. vanilla extract

2 cups all-purpose flour

2 tsp. ground cinnamon

1 tsp. baking soda

1 tsp. table salt

2½ lb. Granny Smith apples (about 4 large), peeled and cut into ¼-inch-thick wedges

1½ cups chopped toasted pecans

Vegetable cooking spray

Browned-Butter Frosting

Fresh Apple Cake

MAKES: 12 TO 15 SERVINGS · **HANDS-ON:** 30 MIN. · **TOTAL:** 2 HOURS

Thinly sliced apples create rich, moist layers of fruit within this cake recipe.

1. Preheat oven to 350°. Stir together butter and next 3 ingredients in a large bowl until blended.

2. Combine flour and next 3 ingredients; add to butter mixture, stirring until blended. Stir in apples and 1 cup pecans. (Batter will be very thick, similar to a cookie dough.) Lightly grease a 13- x 9-inch pan with cooking spray. Pour batter into pan.

3. Bake at 350° for 45 minutes or until a wooden pick inserted in center comes out clean. Cool completely in pan on a wire rack (about 45 minutes). Spread Browned-Butter Frosting over top of cake; sprinkle with remaining ½ cup pecans.

NOTE: *Total time does not include preparing frosting.*

Browned-Butter Frosting

Cook 1 cup butter in a small heavy saucepan over medium heat, stirring constantly, 6 to 8 minutes or until butter begins to turn golden brown. Remove pan from heat immediately, and pour butter into a small bowl. Cover and chill 1 hour or until butter is cool and begins to solidify. Beat butter at medium speed with an electric mixer until fluffy; gradually add 1 (16-oz.) package powdered sugar alternately with ¼ cup milk, beginning and ending with powdered sugar. Beat mixture at low speed until well blended after each addition. Stir in 1 tsp. vanilla. Makes about 3½ cups.

Sweet Potato Sheet Cake

MAKES: 24 SERVINGS · **HANDS-ON:** 25 MIN. · **TOTAL:** 2 HOURS, 5 MIN.

With the rich ingredient pair, bacon and sweet potato, your guests will never guess that this cake started with a boxed mix!

1. Preheat oven to 350°. Lightly grease a 13- x 9-inch pan with cooking spray or shortening.

2. Beat cake mix and next 5 ingredients at low speed with an electric mixer 30 seconds. Beat at medium speed 2 minutes. Pour batter into prepared pan.

3. Bake at 350° for 34 to 38 minutes or until a wooden pick inserted in center comes out clean. Cool in pan on wire rack 10 to 15 minutes; remove from pan to wire rack, and cool completely (about 1 hour).

4. Spread top of cake with frosting; sprinkle with toasted pecans. Store covered in refrigerator.

Bacon-Cream Cheese Frosting

Beat 1 (8-oz.) package softened cream cheese and ¼ cup softened butter at medium speed with an electric mixer 2 minutes or until creamy. Beat in 2½ cups powdered sugar, ⅔ cup brown sugar, and ½ tsp. vanilla. Stir in 7 cooked and crumbled bacon slices.

Quick Bite

This recipe would also make wonderfully decadent cupcakes. Just follow baking directions on cake mix package for cupcakes.

INGREDIENTS

Vegetable cooking spray
or shortening

1 (15.25-oz.) box yellow cake mix

¾ cup milk

⅓ cup vegetable oil

3 large eggs

1½ cups mashed cooked
sweet potatoes

1½ tsp. apple pie spice

Bacon-Cream Cheese Frosting

½ cup coarsely chopped
toasted pecans

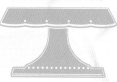

INGREDIENTS

Shortening

2½ cups all-purpose flour

¾ tsp. baking powder

½ tsp. baking soda

½ tsp. table salt

1⅔ cups packed dark brown sugar

1 cup butter, softened

3 large eggs

3 tsp. vanilla extract

¾ cup buttermilk

Simple Rum Frosting

1 cup coarsely chopped toasted pecans

Brown Sugar-Rum Cake

MAKES: 18 SERVINGS • **HANDS-ON:** 20 MIN. • **TOTAL:** 1 HOUR, 55 MIN.

1. Preheat oven to 350°. Grease (with shortening) and lightly flour a 13- x 9-inch pan. Mix flour, baking powder, baking soda, and salt in a medium bowl; set aside.

2. Beat brown sugar and butter at medium speed with an electric mixer until light and fluffy. Add eggs, 1 at a time, beating well after each addition. Beat in vanilla. Alternately add flour mixture and buttermilk to butter mixture, beginning and ending with flour mixture. Beat at low speed just until blended after each addition. Pour batter into prepared pan.

3. Bake at 350° for 32 to 35 minutes or until a wooden pick inserted in center comes out clean. Cool in pan on wire rack 10 to 15 minutes; remove from pan to wire rack, and cool completely (about 1 hour).

4. Spread top of cake with frosting; sprinkle with pecans.

Simple Rum Frosting

Beat 3 cups powdered sugar and ¾ cup softened butter at medium speed with an electric mixer until light and fluffy. Beat in 2 Tbsp. rum.

Quick Bite

Just 2 Tbsp. of rum in the frosting gives this whole cake a burst of flavor. For a nonalcoholic version, substitute Cream Cheese Frosting (page 43).

Index

Metric Equivalents

The recipes that appear in this cookbook use the standard U.S. method for measuring liquid and dry or solid ingredients (teaspoons, tablespoons, and cups). The information on this chart is provided to help cooks outside the United States successfully use these recipes. All equivalents are approximate.

Metric Equivalents for Different Types of Ingredients

A standard cup measure of a dry or solid ingredient will vary in weight depending on the type of ingredient. A standard cup of liquid is the same volume for any type of liquid. Use the following chart when converting standard cup measures to grams (weight) or milliliters (volume).

Standard Cup	Fine Powder (ex. flour)	Grain (ex. rice)	Granular (ex. sugar)	Liquid Solids (ex. butter)	Liquid (ex. milk)
1	140 g	150 g	190 g	200 g	240 ml
3/4	105 g	113 g	143 g	150 g	180 ml
2/3	93 g	100 g	125 g	133 g	160 ml
1/2	70 g	75 g	95 g	100 g	120 ml
1/3	47 g	50 g	63 g	67 g	80 ml
1/4	35 g	38 g	48 g	50 g	60 ml
1/8	18 g	19 g	24 g	25 g	30 ml

Useful Equivalents for Dry Ingredients by Weight

(To convert ounces to grams, multiply the number of ounces by 30.)

1 oz	=	1/16 lb	=	30 g
4 oz	=	1/4 lb	=	120 g
8 oz	=	1/2 lb	=	240 g
12 oz	=	3/4 lb	=	360 g
16 oz	=	1 lb	=	480 g

Useful Equivalents for Length

(To convert inches to centimeters, multiply the number of inches by 2.5.)

1 in			=	2.5 cm		
6 in	=	1/2 ft	=	15 cm		
12 in	=	1 ft	=	30 cm		
36 in	=	3 ft	= 1 yd	=	90 cm		
40 in			=	100 cm	=	1 m

Useful Equivalents for Liquid Ingredients by Volume

1/4 tsp					=	1 ml
1/2 tsp					=	2 ml
1 tsp					=	5 ml
3 tsp	=	1 Tbsp			=	1/2 fl oz	=	15 ml
		2 Tbsp	=	1/8 cup	=	1 fl oz	=	30 ml
		4 Tbsp	=	1/4 cup	=	2 fl oz	=	60 ml
		5 1/3 Tbsp	=	1/3 cup	=	3 fl oz	=	80 ml
		8 Tbsp	=	1/2 cup	=	4 fl oz	=	120 ml
		10 2/3 Tbsp	=	2/3 cup	=	5 fl oz	=	160 ml
		12 Tbsp	=	3/4 cup	=	6 fl oz	=	180 ml
		16 Tbsp	=	1 cup	=	8 fl oz	=	240 ml
		1 pt	=	2 cups	=	16 fl oz	=	480 ml
		1 qt	=	4 cups	=	32 fl oz	=	960 ml
						33 fl oz	=	1000 ml	=	1 l

ISBN-13: 978-0-8487-0298-4
ISBN-10: 0-8487-0298-0
Library of Congress Control Number: 2014933368
Printed in the United States of America
Fourth Printing 2016

The Southern Cake Book

Editor: Allison E. Cox
Senior Designer: J. Shay McNamee
Executive Food Director: Grace Parisi
Assistant Test Kitchen Manager: Alyson Moreland Haynes
Recipe Developers and Testers: Wendy Ball, R.D.;
 Tamara Goldis, R.D.; Stefanie Maloney; Callie Nash;
 Karen Rankin; Leah Van Deren
Food Stylists: Victoria E. Cox; Margaret Monroe Dickey,
 Catherine Crowell Steele
Photography Director: Jim Bathie
Senior Photographer: Hélène Dujardin
Senior Photo Stylist: Kay E. Clarke
Photo Stylist: Mindi Shapiro Levine
Assistant Photo Stylist: Mary Louise Menendez
Senior Production Manager: Sue Chodakiewicz
Assistant Production Manager: Diane Rose Keener

Contributors

Project Editor: Melissa Brown
Designer: Amy Bickell
Compositor: Frances Higginbotham
Copy Editors: Rhonda Lother, Rebecca Benton
Proofreader: Julie Bosche
Indexer: Nanette Cardon
Fellows: Ali Carruba, Elizabeth Laseter, Amy Pinney,
 Madison Taylor Pozzo, Deanna Sakal, April Smitherman,
 Megan Thompson, Tonya West
Food Stylist: Ana Price Kelly
Photographer: Becky Luigart-Stayner
Photo Stylists: Fonda Shaia, Leslie Simpson

Southern Living

Editor: M. Lindsay Bierman
Creative Director: Robert Perino
Managing Editor: Candace Higginbotham
Executive Editors: Hunter Lewis, Jessica S. Thuston
Deputy Food Director: Whitney Wright
Test Kitchen Director: Robby Melvin
Test Kitchen Specialist/Food Styling: Vanessa McNeil Rocchio
Test Kitchen Professionals: Pam Lolley
Recipe Editor: JoAnn Weatherly
Style Director: Heather Chadduck Hillegas
Director of Photography: Jeanne Dozier Clayton
Photographers: Robbie Caponetto, Laurey W. Glenn,
 Hector Sanchez
Assistant Photo Editor: Kate Phillips Robertson
Photo Coordinator: Chris Ellenbogen
Senior Photo Stylist: Buffy Hargett Miller
Assistant Photo Stylist: Caroline M. Cunningham
Photo Administrative Assistant: Courtney Authement
Editorial Assistant: Pat York